REFLECTIONS OF A CATHOLIC PRIEST

Fr. Glenn Kohrman

authorHOUSE®

AuthorHouse™
1663 Liberty Drive, Suite 200
Bloomington, IN 47403
www.authorhouse.com
Phone: 1-800-839-8640

First published by AuthorHouse 9/30/2008

ISBN: 978-1-4343-5811-0 (sc)

Printed in the United States of America
Bloomington, Indiana

This book is printed on acid-free paper.

To Bonz

My mother

God Rest Her Gentle Soul

ACKNOWLEDGMENTS

I would like to thank God for any good that comes from this work, and many others who have contributed to the completion of this project. My parents and my family have been a great blessing for me. My immediate family includes: Deb and Ed Schmieman, Becky and Bob Kawiecki, Amy and Jim Breckler, Jerry and Ginny Kohrman, Brad and Brenda Kohrman, Richard and Judy Kohrman, and Michelle and Jay Kennedy. My family has always been a great support to me and special thanks to those who have read the manuscript at the early stages. I would like to give special thanks to Jeff Kenney, a very sharp guy and a generous spirit who did careful proofreading of the text and offered some great suggestions. I also truly appreciate the contribution of Mimi Weirick and Joan McClure who also read the text and also provided great recommendations. My niece also did some corrections and suggested the title so thanks to Beth Breckler too! Also thanks to Fr. Thom Lombardi and Joe Rulli who also read the text and encouraged me to complete the project.

CONTENTS

About the Author

I was born in Fort Wayne, Indiana and grew up in a small neighboring town called New Haven. I was the product of two years of Catholic Education, first and second grade. I was taught in those years by some sisters of St. Agnes. Following there, I went to a public elementary school and public high school. I wrestled my freshman year, went out for tennis and was cut, and then ran track from my sophomore year, throwing the shot and discus. My senior year I played football on a team that was undefeated in the regular season. My first jobs included sweeping floors after hours in a clothing manufacturing facility and being a Park Maintenance worker. This entailed getting ball diamonds ready to play and keeping the grass cut in all the township parks. As a senior in high school I was accepted in an engineering cooperative program at a plant that manufactured oil seals in Van Wert, Ohio.

My college started with two years at the extension of Purdue University at Fort Wayne. Affectionately known then as "By-pass High", the campus was located on the bypass around Fort Wayne. My junior and senior college years were on campus in West Lafayette. There I completed a Bachelor's Degree in Mechanical Engineering. Near the end of my under-graduate studies, a professor approached me and asked if I would be interested in a research assistantship to obtain a Masters Degree in Mechanical Engineering. Ironically, among my college friends I was one who usually complained the loudest about school. I had no fondness for school, but I certainly liked to learn and figure out things.

One of the reasons I went into engineering was to test an idea I had for a high mileage gasoline carburetor. It wasn't until my junior year in a class of Thermodynamics that I determined my 1973 Dodge Charger should theoretically get 73 miles per gallon, going 55 miles per hour, assuming an adiabatic efficiency of 17% and the caloric value of gasoline being 128,000 BTU's per gallon!

The research at Purdue for the Masters Degree was funded as the result of a grant from the Ford Motor Company. I accepted and finished the basic course work and defended my thesis in May, 1987 and officially received my Masters Degree in Mechanical Engineering with an emphasis on acoustics in December of 1987.

Near the end of my studies at Purdue, while in a Christian dating relationship with a fine Christian woman, I felt drawn to consider the priesthood. I entered St. John's Seminary in Boston in September, 1987. I finished my theological course work in May, 1992 and was ordained for the diocese of Fort Wayne-South Bend in Indiana in November of that year. In the following years I completed a thesis in Systematic Theology on the Interpretation of Scripture which fulfilled the requirements for a Masters of Arts Degree in Theology.

My first pastoral assignments entailed service as a deacon in Bradford, MA at Sacred Hearts parish and then St. Michael's in Plymouth, Indiana. During my assignment at Plymouth I finished teaching a class at Ancilla College in Ethics. The priest who had been teaching the course was unable to finish the class as the result of some serious problems. As a priest I spent my first fourteen months at the parish of St. Mary's of the Assumption in Decatur, Indiana as an associate pastor. I also served as a part-time chaplain to Bishop Luer's High School in Fort Wayne, Indiana. Then in the summer of 1994 I was named administrator of two inner city parishes, Sacred Heart and St. Paul's. St. Paul's was a predominately Hispanic parish. Unfortunately now the property is merely a grassy knoll. The Spanish parishioners were moved to St. Patrick's some years after I left St. Paul's. In August of 1998 I left Sacred Heart and became pastor of St. Patrick's in Fort Wayne as the result of the untimely death of St. Patrick's pastor. I continued to serve St. Paul's which had grown from around 160 families on the books to over 800 in the summer of 2001. In August, 2001 I was named pastor of St. Mary of the Lake in Culver, Indiana, a small rural parish that also had the responsibility of serving Culver Academies in Culver, Indiana as Catholic Chaplain. Culver Academies is a very interesting place. Students come from more than 20 countries from all over the world, and Culver Academies does its best to fashion future citizens for the world. Also, since the summer of 2002 I have been an Adjunct Faculty member of Ancilla College teaching Ethics, Philosophy and other courses in Religious Studies and even a course in College Algebra. In the spring of 2006 I also taught a class on the New Testament at the University of St. Francis in Fort Wayne, Indiana.

INTRODUCTION

As a priest there are many things that compel one to reflect on life's meaning and its deeper truth. What makes us tick? What makes others tick? What does give life its meaning? These are not easy questions, but hopefully these reflections, if nothing else will help one to ponder these deep questions more thoroughly.

I can remember hearing the story of *The Emperor's New Clothes* which may serve as a good image to reflect on the difficulties that we find in today's culture. The general idea of the story is summarized below:

> *One day an emperor decided that he would dress quite differently than had been his custom. He lived in a civilized world and his subjects have been conditioned to be respectful, and to avoid being offensive at all costs. The emperor exercising his leadership role enters wearing his "new clothes", which in reality were no clothes at all. All his subjects swoon at the emperor's "insight", and "openness" and ingenuity. One of the youngest members of the kingdom points out that the emperor's new clothes are not clothes at all. In fact, he was simply naked!*

Fortunately, as I recall, the king was humble enough to recognize the truth when he heard it!

This book is not meant to be a tirade against the evils of the world or a moralizing work that assails a valueless culture spinning out of control. Rather, I hope to provide some reflections on life as a priest, the world, and what it really takes to be a survivor, both now and for all eternity, and indeed why I am giving my life to the ministerial priesthood of Jesus Christ as understood in the Roman Catholic Church and her authoritative teaching. The essence of priesthood is to bring Christ into the world. Literally and really to bring the Real Presence of Jesus Christ, His Body, Blood, Soul and Divinity into the earthly plain - this is the mission of the priest

Our western culture seems to be moving so fast that it is very difficult to slow down enough to think about those things that truly matter; namely: life, love and truth, not to mention faith which can help us sort out some of the most thorny issues of life. I am convinced that at the heart of true happiness and being a real survivor in this life are found indeed, love and truth and faith! To experience humanity most fully, a person must come to grips with who they are and how to live as the result of such self-knowledge.

It seems that the psychological community is also coming around to value such things. This new field, yet very old in light of the Church, is what the secular world is beginning to call positive psychology. I don't have the source for it, but I was told that a leader at a conference of psychiatrists began to question some of their approaches. It seems that people in general are getting less mentally healthy than more so. His proposal was to focus on good behavior as opposed to bad behavior. In other words virtue is now becoming popular and in fact Plato, Aristotle, Augustine and Thomas Aquinas were suggested as viable sources to reflect on what should be considered good behavior. This would not surprise G.K. Chesterton who noted that what drew him to the Catholic Church was not the fact that the Church was right when he was right, but that the Church proved to be right when he was wrong! This is said as seemingly only Chesterton can say it.[1]

Before a person can find anything, a person has to know what one is looking for, and if one is mistaken in his or her perceptions, he or she will only become further confused or further from his or her goal. How many scientists are convinced of their respective hypotheses, only to discover that they were incorrect? In one sense they are indeed closer to the truth because they have excluded one possibility, but in another sense they are not much closer to finding

1 The Catholic Church, On my Conversion, G. K. Chesterton.

the true solution to their query. Only if we are fortunate enough to be looking in the right direction will we ever find the truth.

Many today believe there is no God, and they make their decision based on their faith in such a proposition. I hope this work can challenge people to have and open mind and come to see faith in God and in His Church as something not so silly.

The first chapter is on religion in general. In particular I think real religion is grounded in truth. Truth is certainly a perennial question, one need look no farther than Pontius Pilate, the Roman procurator who is reported to be the one who opened the way for the crucifixion of Jesus Christ. Pilate's words ring out through history, "truth, truth what does that mean?" There is a discussion on aspects of myth and how it must never be confused with truth claims. There is also some reflection on what some past thinkers have said on truth, from Augustine to Wittgenstein. On the myth side of things mention is made of Dan Brown Joseph Campbell and J.R.R. Tolkien.

On some level every person is looking for purpose and meaning in their life. I felt as though I may be able to make some contribution in helping others reflect on those things in life that give it purpose and meaning and how religion fits into the mix. I believe that one can embrace faith without abandoning reason. Faith is essential, but it is not alone in coming to recognize the fullness of truth in God. Augustine's dictum is helpful here, "*faith seeking understanding*". I would like to think there is a little food for thought in this chapter. I would argue that at the heart of any religion is its claims it makes on truth and ultimately how it is distinct from myth. True religion is not a myth; it is very far from it indeed. I would even go so far as to say that this is the fundamental problem with secular intellectuals; they believe that religion is ultimate myth.

We all have a history. The second chapter deals with an account of Salvation History and in some sense our intellectual history. We humans are all in this together, and I am a firm believer that there are experiences or events, even ordeals, that go beyond culture and individuals. I believe that we can actually learn from each other, and that there are indeed meaningful things to learn. One can look at two fundamental approaches when looking at history. The first being one that is agnostic if not even atheistic, H.G. Wells takes such an approach in his <u>History of Man</u>; G.K Chesterton would accept the premise that something was behind all this, his account is found in, <u>The Everlasting Man</u>. This chapter considers the difference and recounts major historical events that have shaped Christianity.

A central aspect of salvation history from the Judeo-Christian perspective revolves around the concept of covenant. A covenant is much more than a contract, it is actually a committed relationship rooted in love. Salvation History is rich with these covenants that God had entered into with the human family. One can look at 6 of these with the 7th to come which may be seen as the way in which God's plan will be fulfilled.

One of the most difficult things for me to accept is that seemingly some people are so slow to even be open to the idea of an objective history that goes beyond their own opinion or perceptions. The truth is rooted in history, if we are honest with ourselves, our experience can lead us to a deep encounter with the truth and take us far beyond any myth and in fact face to face with the One.

The third chapter is a reflection on the priesthood. The priesthood is a way in which the real presence of Christ can be experienced in the world. As I see it, Jesus' ultimate mission was simply to glorify the Father, and to do this He made it possible that we might be one in Him, as He is one in the Father. (See John 17:20) Within the last week of starting this introduction, I have had the opportunity to officiate the funeral of the mother of a friend. She died of Lou Gehrig's disease. I am waiting on a call from a family whose child has just been diagnosed with a serious genetic defect and is not expected to live. There are things that happen in life that have no fully satisfying answer from a merely human perspective. There is pain, tragedy, heartache and frustration, but with this strange thing called faith, I truly believe one can make at least some sense of those sufferings that seem so incomprehensible; on the other side of life, its great joys too can be understood.

Priests have the privilege of being present at very big moments in people's lives. When people fall in love, and they love each other so much they want to give themselves to each other in a public way, a priest is there. When new life from the grace of baptism is given to children, Christ is made present in those encounters as well. When people die the priest is there to proclaim a message of hope in the face of mourning and sorrow. A priest at the moment of such tragedies and joys is doing Christ's work, the priest in a very unique way has the opportunity to bring Christ to those situations of loss, suffering, pain and joy.

We could hardly talk about the priesthood without some reflection on the recent scandals in the Church. As the new millennium passed many allegations had surfaced and indeed some priests had been credibly charged for horrible crimes against children. When this broke John Paul II was quick to call this a betrayal of "the grace of Ordination in succumbing even to the most grievous forms of the 'mysterium iniquitatis' at work in the world"[2]. These crimes, principally against young teenage boys, though in even very rare situations against very young children, are seen by the Church as not only sinful, but a crime. This has led many to attack the institution and the Church's discipline of celibacy, as opposed to the real problem, namely sin in the world. Sin, interestingly enough, is defined by the Catholic Church as "offense against reason, truth and right judgment".[3] Crimes against children are indeed all of that!

A good priest really is a "father", not to be confused with "The Father". This chapter also reflects on the dimensions of fatherhood and the exclusive demands it makes on the person. There is discussion on priestly celibacy and how this has been a general rule, though not an exclusive one, from apostolic times. From a Catholic perspective Jesus glorifies the Father through the legacy of the Sacraments and the ministry of God's holy people, certainly this ministry is not limited to the priest, but is certainly made uniquely present in the priest's ministry.

The fourth chapter takes a look at the world. Also as I began this work, the culture was enamored with "Reality TV". From shows such as "Who wants to be a Millionaire", "Survivor" and "The Weakest Link", and a plethora of others that seem to reduce relationships to nothing more than sexual gratification, or physical beauty, or to embrace material wealth as the ultimate goal. It seems

---

2 Letter to Priests for Holy Thursday 2002.

3 Catechism of the Catholic Church, n. 1849.

to me that the ideals or values which I would judge to give life real meaning are truly lacking in each of these shows. They contribute to an illusion and distort what truly matters. Sadly much of our world is driven by such illusions. Everyone, whether they admit it or not, lives by some kind of faith, faith in themselves, faith in nature, or even faith in no thing. Faith can be a very dangerous thing. If people put their faith in things that are not the fullness of truth, they can find themselves flying jet planes into buildings. It is for this reason that our faith is not devoid of reason, but rather transcends or supercedes it, at the same time not contradicting it.

The world seems to operate under its own assumptions or even illusions. There is a real tendency towards myth building. Generally it claims to be guided by science, but the world has not had a great track record. Great minds often see things differently, whether it be the world renowned physicist, Steven Hawking or Albert Einstein. Assumptions are always at work and that sometimes has led to disastrous consequences.

Chapter five relates to the family and what is deemed to be its politically correct derivatives. The family is key to having a peaceful and loving society. When society fails to support the family or individuals fail to respect each other great evil typically results. The thing that principally and most importantly gives significance or meaning to life is a deep and profound respect for human dignity. If we are respected, we have a lot. The man who senselessly killed the individuals and himself at Virginia Tech blamed his actions on not being respected as a child. Clearly not all children who are made fun end up as mass murderers. The important point is that if we can truly grow in our respect for others, and others respect us, the world will be much better for it. There are many things that people think will bring happiness. What if you have a million dollars and no one to share it with? Or if you manage to "survive" while all others have been alienated and thus leave you in total isolation? Or what if strength is judged merely on intellectual prowess, or beauty or externals? Is this not an incredibly shallow view of life? Will it not lead to discontent, isolation and maybe even despair? The world's view of family is often self-serving and will lead to self-destruction.

Chapter six discusses in detail John Paul II's understanding of the family and how important it is for humanity's future. The telling observation is "All of humanity passes by way of the family".

Chapter seven turns to a reflection on evil and its devastating effects. The day September 11, 2001 will be another day that lives in infamy; a day when some profoundly misguided individuals, presumably faith filled (as wrong-headed as their particular and individual understanding of the Islamic faith was) hi-jacked four jumbo jets loaded with fuel and were "successful" in reaching three of their targets, the two World Trade Towers in New York and the Pentagon. The fourth attempt was believed to be thwarted by heroic acts by some passengers on board one of the ill-fated hijacked planes. These attacks changed our world. There were seemingly new opportunities for collaboration and relationships that heretofore seemed impossible. This event alone, at least at the onset, seemed to have awakened in the great human spirit those things that are most important. Sadly as time has passed the event is used or misused as a non-pivotal event. War is always a loss for humanity as was so eloquently stated by John Paul II. The sad reality is that you have corrupt regimes that profit by war, hatred and misinformation.

In Chapter eight I will spend some time in the following pages on the mystery of suffering. John Paul II, after he was shot, reflected on the Christian Meaning of Human Suffering in his apostolic letter, *Salvifici Doloris*.[4] Suffering is an experience the human person cannot escape. Suffering has driven many to despair and others to heroic acts of virtue and self sacrifice. The words of Bishop Fulton Sheen are also memorable. Paraphrasing, they are something like, "Suffering without Christ is nothing but misery, but when we are able to unite our sufferings with His (when we are able to offer them up), we participate in the redemption of the world!" This simple phrase, "offer it up" which has been so prevalent in the Catholic tradition, is so rich and deeply meaningful if we are to live in the world of reality and not illusion. The Hebrew Scriptures tells us that God creates

---

4 The Vatican Web Site address is: http://www.vatican.va/holy_father/john_paul_ii/apost_letters/documents/hf_jp_ii_apl_11021984_salvifici_doloris_en.html

out of nothing. God can also reveal to us untold marvels through the suffering we endure and turn over to Him.

Chapter nine reflects on the essence of what we are, we are good. Goodness and truth go together. Truth is humanity's only hope - not technology, not ingenuity - but truth which ultimately leads to better technology and ingenuity. If, however, technology will not submit to sound ethical and moral principles, technology will lead to the degradation of the human person and more deeply entrench the culture of death in our daily lives.

Chapter ten reflects on John Paul II's document on the Splendor of Truth. Truth has its splendor, it leads to technological insight and ultimately insight into moral truths that will protect humanity even from itself if the truths are embraced and practiced.

Chapter eleven reflects on that which I think is key to building a world of peace. At the heart of the solution is a respect for human dignity and at the heart of human dignity is respect for religious liberty. Faith and love are very similar in that they can only truly be meaningful when they are practiced in freedom.

Chapter twelve reflects on the significance of fatherhood as it relates to the priesthood. I believe it is only in this dimension that one can make sense out of the male priesthood. Priesthood must never be understood in terms of power, but rather service.

Finally the reflection concludes with the importance of the various dimensions of the priesthood and its demands. If we truly want to discover the truth, we must be willing to engage in its pursuit. You will not find something if you are unwilling or unable to look for it. A fundamental problem exists when we even bring up the word "truth". Truth is something we all want, but few seem willing to be subject to its constraints. Truth, in my understanding of it, does not depend on me. In other words, if a tree falls in the woods, it <u>does</u> make a sound, *even if I am not there to hear it, or anyone for that matter.* This is where common sense comes in. If the tree falls, the bunny rabbit will jump, even if no one is there to see it jump. Reality simply is as it is. Particular people can have erroneous opinions, but wrong opinions have no bearing on the truth. Truth does not depend on what a person believes. People can be wrong. I can be wrong. But that also means that I can be right!

When we fail to follow the truth, we set ourselves up for great disappointment and maybe even our own destruction. I often say, "While God always forgives, nature never forgives!" I have some experience in piloting small aircraft. If a person is distracted while taking off or landing and the plane falls below the stall speed, and if the plane is too close to the ground, the plane will crash. God will forgive the person's lack of attentiveness, but the person will be dead nonetheless. This will be the result, regardless of one's intention or one's belief that the plane was not experiencing a stall!

The purpose of my reflections is simple: while there is so much to read and so many things to learn, my hope is that all who read this book may come to appreciate how valuable they are as individuals, along with how valuable every human being is, even those who are enemies to the truth. If they make this realization, they will not be enemies of the truth or the church for long! My hope is that those who see the Church as antiquated or even intellectually dishonest will come to see the truth as it is and not continue to be blinded by pride and sin, and ultimately by wrong-headed, philosophical presuppositions

Finally the Epilogue reflects on some of Pope Benedict's insights from his papal documents, namely *Deus Caritas* Est, *God is Love*, some of the incidents that occurred during the early stages of his pontificate, such as the flap over the Rosegburg Lecture, his comments regarding salvation and other Christian communities, and some of his insights from his book *Jesus of Nazareth*.

God is the "object" of our faith. God is about love and Love animates our faith, a faith that will move us to act in such a way that our world will be a much better place and we will be much happier for it.

CHAPTER I · WHAT IS RELIGION?

A reflection on the priesthood could hardly begin without first addressing the concept of religion in general. When we talk about religion in our contemporary world, the concept of myth as it is found in contemporary circles needs to be addressed as well. Most people, when they hear the word "myth", think of fairy tales or at the very least stories having nothing to do with historical fact. In their best light, myths are seen to be true in a qualified sense. The truth is manifest through "symbolic" language in the technical sense of the word.

There are excellent examples of myth in its true sense and also clear distinctions regarding myth and the Judeo-Christian accounts. J.R.R. Tolkien and his works, *The Hobbit*, and *The Lord of the Ring Trilogy*, is an excellent example of myth genre in its pure form. Without belaboring the topic, I would also refer the reader to G.K. Chesterton's, The Everlasting Man. It truly is helpful in confronting the contemporary attempts at dismissing the Christian understanding of salvation by perceiving it as merely a myth among other equally "valid" myths. I suggest that there is something singularly unique in the Christian story. Properly speaking I believe the Judeo-Christian story is truly the History of the Human Person's salvation. In one sense the narrative continues to be written as we speak, or shall I say, "act". I do not find it helpful to speak of the Judeo-Christian creation accounts in terms of myth as it is commonly understood. By the same token, if one understands myth in a qualified sense, it still can be a way to discuss the Christian faith. It seems that it would be fair to place some of the early Christian apocryphal writings in the category of myth (e.g. *The Gospel of Judas*). It is a little ironic that many will look at some of these non-historical writings and treat them as more historically accurate than the biblical accounts themselves (e.g. The DaVinci Code). They often become fodder for Hollywood because Hollywood seems to be more attuned to its particular agendas that I suspect are more underlying than intentional. Hollywood thrives on illusion, and humans seem to love illusions.

There was a popular series of books in Christian circles in the 80's and 90's, the first of the series being a book called Joshua. Joshua in Hebrew means "Savior". In Greek the name that would reflect this meaning is Jesus. The series focuses on the character Joshua, who is compassionate and clearly politically correct. It would seem, according to this book, that all religions are seen as equal in God's sight, and no one seems to be wrong. In fact, at one point the author looks at the etymology for the word "religion" and erroneously characterizes it to come from the roots that suggest "to bind up". In reality the word religion, broken down, comes from "re" which means "again" and "ligion" which has its roots from the word that means "to connect". So it would seem a better explanation for the word is "to bind or to connect *again*". Therefore in its true sense religion is the means which one has to reconnect to God or that higher power after the resulting fracture or broken relationship has occurred.

This popular series of books is not alone in putting forth the idea that all religions are basically the same. The Fraternal Order of Masons would also seem to suggest that all religion is good and that no one religion can be seen as better than another. In other words, the implication seems to be that it would make no sense to try and find the true religion because if it would exist, it merely is impossible to determine which religion could make that claim. Again, this is driven by the philosophical pre-supposition that ultimately "truth cannot be known". Implicit in this may be the claim that religion need not be true in terms of historical fact, but rather something that is at least not bad for society. This view is at least far superior than the view that many intellectuals seem to ascribe to today, namely that religion is truly a scourge on humanity, something to be tolerated, e.g. "religious tolerance". They point to the history of religious wars and violence, all done in the name of religion. We need to look no farther than the War on Terror that began this millennium; a war that began as the result of presumed Islamic extremists against what they considered to be the infidels or the decadent West. In reality, credible testimonies allege that the suicide bombers are driven more by political ideologies that instill a sense of hopelessness and feel that this is their only way to effect political change. Again it would seem that a true understanding of religion is not the root cause, but rather can hopefully lead to a real solution.

I pose that religion is often used solely as a pretense to further ideologies and political agendas. The tragic irony: over 2000 died as the result of that terrorist extremism, and nearly 4000 unborn children are killed a day - yes every day - as the result of pre-born children having no right to life. These children die as the result of the extreme abortion policies in the United States. The facts are staggering: about one out of every three pregnancies ends in abortion. Those who worked at the Twin Towers had much better odds than those who are being conceived today. It begs the question: who are more confused, or more villainous in their extremism? These extremists share the same delusion that human life is expendable and has no significant value, unless of course you believe a certain way or have the power to choose.

I am somewhat amazed by such a perspective when one considers the devastation done by those who had the *enlightened* view that held that religion had no significance and in fact was an enemy of the state. If you need something to jog the memory, consider Hitler, Lenin, and Stalin; certainly these madmen were not driven by religious idealism. In fact, they were driven by an ideology that was devoid of religion. They saw power as their god and people as merely things to be manipulated, controlled and dominated by those in power. Those who embrace secular ideals today are quick to approve human experimentation on genetically complete humans and adopt eugenic polices that are making judgments, not based on the infinite value of the individual, but rather on what seems good for most people. In other words, many adopt a radical pragmatism which in the past has been used to justify slavery and a host of other terrible injustices.

Many religions can boldly make the claim that their particular understanding is the truth, and in reality I believe that all legitimate religions are grounded in the truth. There are profoundly good aspects or dimensions in all world religions and even philosophical systems that would not even consider themselves as religions as such. There must be profound respect of people's religious liberty. Dialogue is essential because we can learn from each other, and if there is hope for the future it lies in developing this profound and deep respect for humans and their beliefs. With that said, I believe that some religions or systems of belief have deeper insight into the actual truth than others, just like some doctors are better than others, or some IT (Information Technology) technicians are better than others. The human person, by his or her nature, longs for life, love and truth. Religion is merely the means through which one comes to appreciate these profound longings of the human heart.

The politically correct position is to suggest that there is no real way of knowing the truth, so it is left to each and every individual to do what he or she thinks is best. The ironic tragedy of this position is that real communication is impossible. If there is no truth, then there can be no possibility of coming to some deeper understanding about anything. Many seem to suggest that there is no way that religion should have any public ramifications. In fact, if an individual sees religion as informing some decision, the individual is often ostracized and judged as an extremist. But what if the position that is being espoused is the truth? Can it still be utilized to benefit humanity? I do not want to belabor the absurd, but in the Judeo-Christian world it is a sin to kill the innocent. Now, if one happens to be a Satanist, killing the innocent is actually a great form to express one's particular "religious devotion", it is obvious that such behavior is not legitimate religious freedom. I think I heard Alan Keys make a simple but profound statement, "we must never have the right to do what is wrong!" It doesn't take a rocket scientist to figure out that this kind of religion is against human interests, or does it? This example is crazy, but there must be limits and the limits must be rooted in Human dignity. Until a cat or a dog or any other life form can write a legal brief or communicate on some clear level, it is up to humans to govern our world and respect life; all life, and in particular, the epitome of life's rational form, the Human Person. The United States was founded to be a country that was free *for* the practice of religion, not to be a country free *from* religious practice.

A key element of religion that seems to cut across cultural boundaries is a sense of sacrifice that is found in essentially all practice of religion. The etymology of the word "sacrifice" literally would have the sense, "to make sacred or holy". What does it mean to be holy? Often this would have the sense meaning to be "set apart", to be "wholly other", to be totally different from other things. For Buddha this would be "enlightenment", for the Christian it would be oneness with God. The mystics would call it divine union with God, the God who created out of nothing.

Alan Bloom, a Jewish philosopher, I believe, once made the statement, "We need an open mind, but not so open that our brain falls out!" Remember the story of the emperor in the Introduction? One of the youngest members of the kingdom was insightful enough to speak the truth as it is. It is important for us to strive for such **common sense**, which, sad to say, does not seem so common today.

All people, by their very nature, are looking for something. It is part of who we are to question and pursue that illusive query concerning the meaning of life. If our basic needs are met, if we are not consumed with trying to merely survive or if we are fortunate enough to live in a place where we do not spend most of our time gathering wood for a fire to boil the water we drink or the food we must cook, and even if we have the ability to read the words on this page, we cannot help but wonder why we exist, or what is the point of life.

Many propose solutions to the meaning of life. Unfortunately it seems wealth or prosperity is often seen as that which will foster happiness or be the only means to achieve it. People selling their wares propose that happiness is found in possessing this thing or that product. I remember an advertisement that suggested capping one's teeth would result in effecting the biggest change one could make in one's life! My goodness, if that is the case, one seems to lack some insight into just how important life is! We as humans are on a quest for happiness, and we will be restless until we find it. I truly believe that those who make it their quest to find happiness will die in a futile search, but those who strive to make others happy will discover just how happy they are!

Religion is a means to satisfy, at least partially, these deep longings of the human heart. Religion can give life meaning and purpose. I believe this to be the case, not just as an academic exercise, but because it is the way the human person discovers what truly matters: namely, the truth! As a person begins this quest for faith, where is he or she to look? There are so many options, who can a person trust? One must consider history, but whose version is one to trust? These are difficult questions, but I think the answers can be narrowed and that some faiths are much easier to accept than others.

I once heard a lecture about truth and religion that I found quite helpful. The speaker used categories that I was unaccustomed to using. He was drawing from some insights from the philosopher, Ludwig Wittgenstein and his work <u>Philosophical Investigations</u>.[5] The speaker suggested that it would be helpful to think in terms of what he called "grammar and practice". To demonstrate his point he used the game of chess as an analogy. Chess is a fairly complex game. The basis of any game is comprised of its object and various rules. Depending on the complexity of the game there also lies a certain strategy or the way one chooses to play the game within the framework of the rules.

The grammar consists of the rules of the game, while its practice lies in the strategy or the way in which one chooses to play the game. The grammar is never open to doubt. To play a game by not following the rules makes it ultimately impossible to play the game. On the other hand, one's particular strategy is always open to doubt. Many people have different strategies. This is evident in chess, but maybe more evident in the game of football. Will one rely on a strong offense or defense, or will one build the team to be a passing team or a running team? It is easy to question which the best way to go is. Strategies can be questioned, a particular strategy is open to doubt. I found this tremendously helpful in thinking about various religions in particular, but also religion in general.

What would be the grammar and practice of religion in general? I believe that all religions have as their object the escape from the <u>mundane</u>, or maybe one could also understand it as transcending

---

5 <u>Philosophical Investigations</u>, Ludwig Wittgenstein, translated by G.E.M. Anscombie, 1953.

the mundane: in other words, escaping or transcending "worldly things." In the revealed religions, those that claim direct revelation from God, (e.g. Jewish, Christian, Islam), this entails a life in heaven, another world, salvation; for the Hindus the change that will be coming via reincarnation; for the Buddhists it seems to be Nirvana, enlightenment, grasping the illusory aspects of this world. In order for persons to practice any religion, they truly are constrained by the world, so they too are constrained by the laws of this world. It is through adherence to rules of the world that a person will be able to get to the object of the respective religions. In other words, true religion is constrained by natural law. I suggest that while the numerous strategies vary greatly even within respective religious traditions, the grammar of true religion is quite universal. One needs to look no further than the broad truths that most religions put forth as ethical standards: do not murder, do not commit adultery, do not steal, etc.

I think that discerning the various dimensions of respective faith traditions merits reflection. Here is where the rubber hits the road, and also where our world has most difficulty. It is one thing to suggest that all people are equal and have infinite worth. This I believe to be true, but it is altogether different to say all the religions are equally valid. This very paragraph has already, I suspect, raised the ire of many. It begs the questions: Does a religion that practices human sacrifice, the ritual abuse of children or deviant sexual misconduct, such as Satanism, merit the same respect as the non-violent pacifist principals of Buddhism? Anyone with any common sense will be able to recognize the basic differences. I think one can use natural law to prove the point. Humans know that rape is somehow wrong and killing innocent human beings is wrong. It is quite obvious. When one applies this to more subtle differences it is more difficult to discern. How does the Mohammad's child bride line up with the constraints of natural law? In all fairness, it could be that he merely legalized the union to protect the orphan. Historical critics could more accurately and honestly reflect on the objective truth of the matter. If this marriage was arranged to protect a vulnerable child from a harsh society, one can make sense of such a legal arrangement, but if sexual relations with an 8 year old were part of the plan, this is clearly wrong! How is one to judge the human sacrifices of the Aztecs? Are they a "good" act? Obviously not! The answer is clear in light of natural law.

Now shifting our thought to some really politically incorrect areas, all aspects of life and good judgment ultimately come back to truth. I believe that all religions have dimensions of the truth. The task at hand is to try and discern which faith is most fully in accord with the truth. Ultimately the individual soul will be judged on its sincere convictions to know and live the truth. St. Augustine made famous the dictum, "faith seeking understanding". If we are thinking well we will only be drawn closer to the One who created us. We must never judge an individual and presume that we are somehow God's agents of condemnation of individual souls. There is a beautiful passage from the book of Wisdom that rebukes temerity:

> *For your might is the source of justice; your mastery over all things makes you lenient to all. For you show your might when the perfection of your power is disbelieved; and in those who know you, you rebuke temerity. But though you are master of might, you judge with clemency, and with much lenience you govern us; for power, whenever you will, attends you. And you taught your people, by these deeds, that those who are just must be kind; and you gave your sons good ground for hope that you would permit repentance for their sins. [Wisdom 12:16-19, NAB]*

This temerity or this self-righteous insolence is what seems to be that which many so-called Christians use to condemn the ignorant. Temerity cannot be confused with our obligation to help others see what is true and good for all, including themselves. We must use our God-given talents to propose truth with the realization that one can never effectively impose it. This truth is often misjudged as intolerance, but in reality it is what we believe to be the key to happiness and deep and abiding joy. This truth will bring true and lasting peace and freedom and help others recognize the wrong and destructive acts that ultimately harm the welfare of individuals and indeed society and the common good.

At the heart of this truth for me is the message of the Gospel, literally the Good News. Often this "good news" is lost in translation or intentionally obscured. Here are a couple of stories that I believe truly shed light on the real essence of the Gospel message. St. Francis is said to have had an encounter with Christ who tells Francis, "until I return I have no arms and legs but yours!" A similar story was recounted by, I believe, a veteran of WWII who came upon a bombed out church with a statue of Jesus with His arms and legs blown off. Near the remains of the statue was a scrawled inscription which read, "I have no arms and legs but yours!" This is the real sentiment of the Church: act as though all depended on you, and pray knowing that ultimately all depends on God! Jesus is truly made present in His people. It is for this reason that when one grasps this message it changes the way the person treats everyone one meets. The central message is that Jesus lives; He came to save us, and continues to save us through those who strive to be one with Him. There is mercy, there is love, and indeed there is truth. People are valuable, people; all people are loved by God.

True religion is the human person's attempt to "reconnect" to God, to become once again in communion with that higher power. True religion offers a new way to live that is free from death and division and hatred, a place where only love reigns.

I believe that the following is a helpful analogy which can contribute to understanding the value of various faiths and the diversity of religious practice. All the various sects or groups or movements that are aimed at "spiritual enlightenment", each religious path, could be seen as a set of tools in a tool box. The tool box is the "brand" while the tools themselves serve to be useful in accomplishing the task at hand. In this case, the tools would be the means to repair the severed relationship that we all experience with God. Every tool box has a unique set of tools, but I would suggest that there is one set of tools that is superior to all the rest. That tool box has more tools than the others and in fact the tools are better, more technologically advanced. The reason why I like this analogy so much is that although a person may have the best set of tools in the world, there is no guarantee that the person knows how to use them! In fact, if someone was to work on my car, I would be less concerned about the tools that he or she possesses and be much more concerned about the prowess or proficiency the person has developed in using the particular set of tools.

I am a priest, a priest in the Catholic Church. After a great deal of study and reflection, I have come to believe that the Catholic Church has the best set of tools available to humanity. By no means does this suggest that Catholics, as individuals, are somehow better than those of other faiths. We need only to look at individuals who have made the claim that they are Catholic (One could include a list of politicians from a small northeastern state that was famous for a caffeinated drink that was thrown into the harbor over 200 years ago, but maybe I should not be specific) . When people publicly claim that they are Catholic, and then in turn fail to champion the cause for the innocent, unborn child, or defend the genetically complete embryo and even support experimentation on these genetically complete humans, such persons cause grave scandal. Those so-called Catholics have failed to grasp what it means to be Catholic. God alone can read hearts. Only God can determine the response of the human soul to His invitation. This invitation is simple, it entails loving others and treating them as the creatures they are, infinitely valuable and worthy of respect. At the heart of the Catholic faith is a deep and profound respect for human dignity.

One of the German philosophers, Feuerbach, suggested that God can be nothing more than man's best perception of Him. In other words God is nothing more than a human person's ideal of God. He takes for granted that there is no "real" God that transcends perception. This is really quite silly if one takes a moment to reflect on it. The things we make, a drinking glass for example, have no awareness of their maker. That maker would be us! If God is the creator, then it seems reasonable to suggest that we too are unable to recognize our creator. We believe, however, that God chose to reveal Himself to the creature that He created to be self-aware. The believer's presupposition is that created beings come from some entity. That reality of being or entity is what we call God, the Creator.

I truly believe that the teachings of the Church are not simply true because the Bible or the pope tells me so. Rather, when it comes to faith, morals, and that truth which is necessary for our salvation, the pope, when speaking "ex-cathedra", is supernaturally protected from making a mistake and the Bible is without fault. Both the narrowly defined gift of infallibility and the Bible are gifts to humanity to guide us to the fullness of truth. This is true through all ages and applicable to all times past, present and future. More simply stated, something is not true because the Church or Bible says so, rather, the Church or Bible says so because it is true! We can speculate all we want about whether or not God exists. Our speculation has ultimately no bearing as to whether or not God exists! In one very real sense, you cannot prove the truth!

I believe it was St. Augustine who said, "there are many who call themselves Catholics, but they are Catholic in name only (for example, any self-professed Catholic who supports abortion or support politicians who do and those who reject the Church's teaching on sexual morality. These persons would not be Catholic in the true sense of the term). Many others who would not consider themselves Catholic, but in reality respond to God's goodness and follow His truth, would be part of the Church because of their implicit response to God. This teaching is clearly reflected in the Dogmatic Constitution on the Church, *Lumen Gentium, nn. 14-16.*

Karl Rahner, a more contemporary theologian who died in the late 70's used the term, "anonymous Christians". Some feel uncomfortable with this phrase, but it seems to point to a deep reality in the Catholic understanding of the faith. The Second Vatican Council in her document *Lumen Gentium* [6] relates the Church's clear teaching on salvation. This teaching was echoed in the more recent document *Dominus Iesus.*[7] In a way, all salvation is through the Catholic Church because Christ is the only means to salvation because Jesus is the Way, the Truth, and the Life. I realize that such a claim is very politically incorrect! Nonetheless, the Church teaches that all those who are sincerely seeking the Truth, and have discovered any dimension of it, have some relationship to Jesus. Therefore they

6 *Lumen Gentium, nn. 14-16, web site address below:* http://www.vatican.va/archive/hist_councils/ii_vatican_council/documents/vat_ii_const_19641121_lumen_gentium_en.html

7 Web site address: http://www.vatican.va/roman_curia/congregations/cfaith/documents/rc_con_cfaith_doc_20000806_dominus_iesus_en.html

are not totally isolated from the truth that will save and set all of humanity free. Believe me, I understand that the previous statement is about as politically incorrect as one can get, but it begs the question: "Is it the truth?" My faith leads me to the conviction that it is. It is awfully inconvenient that we cannot breathe underwater, but it is the truth. My faith compels me to accept the freedom of all others to either accept or reject the tenants of my faith.

The politically correct position seems to suggest that all faiths are coterminous; in other words, there is no difference between the various religions. Let us state it another way, all religions equally express the inner person's desire for transcendence or even an immanent understanding of God's presence within. Seemingly religion is so personal that one need not be concerned about its precepts at all. In fact, in the United States religion has been characterized as so non-essential that anything that has any religious connotation cannot be part of the public forum. Hence, for example, no manger scenes on public property, even though this represents a historical event that a large segment of the population would recognize as such. One court even went so far as to suggest that the line in the Pledge of Allegiance, "one nation under God", is endorsing religion. I am utterly amazed at the lack of common sense! Our culture has become so confused that pagan feasts are promoted as such, (e.g. Halloween) and in reality, these celebrations or observances have as many religious connotations to some pagan religions as the nativity scene has to Christianity. The hypocrisy is monumental.

In light of September 11th and the terrorist attacks, there does seem to be a reawakening of religious realties. There seems to be a more common-sense view of the world in general, but there is no way to tell if this view will endure. It will be difficult to assess the lasting impact of these horrific events. One thing is for certain: the world has taken a new turn.

I believe in One God, and this God is constantly pursuing us and inviting us to know Him. He chooses usually to speak to us through the ordinary mechanisms of life and daily events. Francis Thomson's poem, *The Hound of Heaven*, relates God's relentless pursuit of the individual. This pursuit is motivated by God's deep and profound love for us. God knows that which is absolutely the best for us, because He made us. If the human person can come to put his trust in God, he will find peace and be on the path to satisfying the deepest longings of the human heart. The person will be truly "religious" (again from the etymology of the word, "*re*" meaning "again" and from *ligion* "to connect or to bind"). The person will be on the path of reconnecting to the only God who can save! He will be practicing true religion.

Does religion stem from Faith alone, or does it make sense?

I for one believe that there is only one way to live life that takes more faith than believing in God, and that would be to live life without faith or belief in God. John Paul II attempts to help one find the means to avoid faith becoming misguided. John Paul II of recent memory had a wonderful reflection on the relationship between faith and reason in *Fides et Ratio*.[8] There is a beautiful quote from the document that poignantly points to this tension between faith and reason while it connects it to the paschal mystery:

> *The preaching of Christ crucified and risen is the reef upon which the link between faith and philosophy can break up, but it is also the reef beyond which the two can set forth upon the boundless ocean of truth. Here we see not only the border between reason and faith, but also the space where the two may meet.*[9]

It is clear that many people today have had their personal reasoning cause shipwreck to their faith, but others have found the way to have it strengthen theirs. I can recall an encounter I had with a clinical psychiatrist at a workshop on ritual abuse. When I was in the seminary I was invited to attend this workshop on the tragic circumstances when individuals have suffered from being brought up in families that practiced the occult. In this situation often people would suffer from extreme personality disorders; sometimes an individual would

8 *Fides et Ratio*, Encyclical Letter of John Paul II, September 14, 1998, http://www.vatican.va/edocs/ENG0216/_INDEX.HTM

9 *ibid, n. 23.*

have nearly 100 different personalities. The psychiatrist in question had been brought up a Catholic, but seemingly lost his faith. In his practice he was asked to help some of these poor souls get their lives back together. After trying his normal course of treatment which seemed to have little effect, he began to wonder about the faith of his youth. As I recall he related that he had one patient who was not responding to any of his treatment, almost in desperation he asked the client to say the name, "Jesus". After some difficulty he was successful, and then also the treatments began to have their effect. Through his practice he had recovered his faith and realized how both faith and psychiatry can go together. In fact it would be a demonstration of how faith and reason are not mutually exclusive but can inform each other.

Faith tells me that this God "thing" is real, and then seemingly God would not give us a brain that He made that would somehow lead us away from Him. Like all things, it is not always easy to become proficient at things. Faith will not give us all the answers, but it does give us the means to face some of the most difficult questions in life. Human suffering is certainly among the greatest of these questions. John Paul II was a man of suffering, and he was a man of faith. We will spend more time on this topic in chapter VIII.

The question of faith confronts all people of all walks of life. I recall from one of our parish faith-sharing groups that one of the participants was distressed because a guest in her home stated that people who are truly intelligent do not believe in God. I liked the response someone gave: "There are really smart people who do not believe and there are really dumb people who don't believe". Likewise there are really smart people who do believe and those who may not have the highest I.Q. who believe as well. It is not unreasonable to believe! The reason why I say this can be demonstrated by a little example which would seemingly be in accord with the second law of thermodynamics, namely the Law of Entropy: reality or events tend towards disorder. Consider a small child's puzzle of perhaps ten pieces. Throw it up in the air one thousand times and count how many times it will land in perfect order. It will not happen! We are infinitely more complex than a ten piece puzzle, and to think that we, as human beings, just randomly fall into place is not very logical! Anyone is free to believe that we are a random accident of nature, but they must have a lot more faith than I do! The problem is that most people will not take the time to reflect on such obvious truths. Many credible scientists conclude that Darwin's theories have too many inconsistencies to be considered an adequate scientific explanation, and yet many seem to be fearful of other explanations of reality, whether it be a simple creation explanation or intelligent design.[10] Again, what then often seems to be common sense is not so common! When we truly acknowledge the existence of God, we are compelled to act on that insight. We change. We realize that there is purpose to this life, and we realize that we truly can be happy. This happiness is not something so much to be found but rather it is to be lived. When a person makes the shift from looking for happiness and instead puts his or her effort in making others happy, he or she has embarked on the path of deep personal satisfaction and fulfillment. This is how the human person is made. We are made to love people and use things, and yet many humans sadly use people and love things. We are made to be lovers of others first. This is the design of the creator. When a person uses a tool incorrectly, it often is deformed or becomes damaged or even useless (e.g. screwdriver as a chisel or pry bar). So when the human person is deceived and hence acts against the natural law or another person, he or she is deeply harmed and damaged.

I am convinced that we live in a culture of unbelief. It may be that some philosophers are not so much against God, but rather that God has become a moot point, something that does not matter. This reminds me of a humorous story. An atheist (literally one who opposes God), and not to be confused with an agnostic (one who simply does not know if God exists or not), who happens to have some scientific knowledge says to God, "I can make anything you can. We have the technology. You have nothing over on us; in fact I can even make a human." God says, "O really?" "Yes I can. Let's have a contest", the atheist says. God agrees! The man is excited, reaches for some dirt to begin his project, and God states, "Get your own dirt. I made this stuff!" Another pithy phrase comes to mind,

---

10 Crisis Magazine, February 2006.

one from Tee Shirt Evangelization: " "God is dead", Nietzsche. "Nietzsche is Dead", God"

Religion is more than a set of ideals that provides a moral code. However, the Catholic faith sees the way to live as discernable just from understanding true human experience. In other words, God's nature manifests they way to live in a way that gives us the fullness of life.

I teach ethics, among other things, at a local junior college. I share with my students on the opening day of class that as hard as it is for them to believe, if I were not a priest, if I were not a Catholic, even if I were not a Christian - I would teach them what follows in the course. Then I let them know that what I will present in this course will make sense, but they must grant me one point. I look one person in the eye (if he or she has blue hair or metal hanging out of his or her head, all the better) and say, "You are infinitely valuable and no one has the right to tell you what to believe or what to think! You okay with that?" Then I say, "Now here is the rub: the person sitting next to you is also infinitely valuable, and no one has the right to tell him or her what to believe or what to think!"

In principle I believe that there is something singularly unique about the human person on earth as we experience him or her. Humans produce technology. Even though dolphins and elephants have "bigger" brains, they do not build cities and machines like we do. True, they have no opposable thumbs, but still ...! So my starting point is that each and every human being has infinite worth. Again the point: each human person is unique and is infinitely valuable. The rub being, the person sitting next to the person is also infinitely valuable. If one believes that, then human dignity becomes the driving force for any ethic that is to be developed.

To develop the point further I challenge the students to consider some scientific dimension that could be used to identify them. Usually it takes the students little time to recognize DNA as a viable and reliable source for identification. I then explain in simple terms how the ova and sperm unite, usually phrased something like, "You have a little ova guy over here and a little sperm guy here, and when they get together you have a genetically complete human being." For the zygote is genetically complete. It may become more than one human if multiple humans develop, but from that point on nothing will develop that is not human. He or she will not be a bunny rabbit or a rat or a grapefruit. He or she will be human, a human who is infinitely valuable, and a human who no one has the right to tell what to believe or what to think.

The corollary to free expression is that we must respect the religious beliefs of every human being, but that would be second to respecting the dignity of the persons themselves. In other words, neither religion nor human progress can ever be the excuse to kill directly or directly harm another innocent human being without the individual's consent. If this point is made clear it then makes sense why a person should not be able to enslave another human being, or abort them, or chemically kill them through contraceptive means or through the embryonic manipulation of some forms of stem cell research or in-vitro fertilization. When life is respected, the Culture of Life is furthered. When it is not, we further the Culture of Death. This culture is epitomized by persons who embrace abortion and research techniques that degrade humanity, and even promote a distorted right to privacy that gives people a license to kill.

My ethics are not merely the result of the Bible telling me what to believe, or even the magisterial pronouncements of the Church informing my approach, but rather a reflection on scientific realities; or in a phrase, natural law. What many fail to grasp in our world is the simple fact that things are not true because the Church teaches them to be so, but rather that the only reason that the Church teaches them is because they are indeed true.

Blaise Pascal presented another challenge to the scientific world of his time. It is often characterized as Pascal's Gamble.[11] I believe Pascal himself would say the following example is not the reason to put faith in God, but he finds it difficult to comprehend why anyone would not believe in God, if they would just take a moment to reflect. It is interesting to note that among Pascal's writings one finds the seminal stages of calculus; he was a scientific genius and at the same time he had a deep faith in God.

Pascal's Gamble reflects four basic possibilities as they relate to God's existence and our response to God's commands. Either the

---

11 Pascal's Thoughts,

Christian God exists or He does not; and we will either follow God's precepts or we will not. Imagine for a moment that God does not exist. If those who believe in God have been deceived and have made the requisite choices in responding to the commands purportedly expressed by this God, then those people may have given up things they need not have given up. They may have experienced less physical pleasure in their lives and had less money to spend on themselves because of their generosity to others. In other words, they have made some limited or finite sacrifices. At the end of their lives, they will die and decompose and adopt the popular cartoon feature, *The Lion King,* and its view concerning the circle of life. Those who choose not to follow God's precepts may have a little more pleasure and more money. This, however, would depend on the level of hedonistic behavior they have chosen to embark upon. Many such choices can lead to venereal disease, or even death or prison. Nonetheless, even if they escape the natural consequences of what Christians call sin, they too will still die and decompose.

The next group of possibilities relates to the true existence of God. If God exists, those who respond to His offer (which entails a finite sacrifice) will merit the infinite gain of eternal life with God and all the joys of Heaven. Those who choose to pursue the finite gains (illicit pleasure, ill gotten gain, etc.) in this life will experience infinite loss and be damned to hell with the devil and his minions. Succinctly put, it would seem more reasonable to make a finite sacrifice at the possibility of an infinite gain, as opposed to a finite gain which could result in an infinite loss.

In less complex terms, can you imagine taking a dollar bill from someone if later on that person could demand from you $1,000,000? Most would be uncomfortable with such a proposition. By the same token, how many are willing to part with a dollar at the prospect of winning the lottery? The stakes are much higher when it comes to eternal salvation or eternal damnation.

The encyclical, *Fides et Ratio,* published by John Paul II on the Triumph of the Cross, September 14, 1997, is a beautiful challenge for us all to think clearly and recognize how philosophy and faith need not be enemies, but rather handmaids to one another. He points out in that document how the relativist, or in the more extreme, the nihilist, is the epitome of closed-mindedness. Philosophies that solely limit themselves to the physical or material dimensions of our experience and take as their presupposition that there can be nothing further than the material world (no supernatural reality) simply are closed-minded. Ironically, a metaphysical-based philosophy, while not presuming the existence of God, is at the very least possibly open to such a contingency. It is the relativist who is ultimately the closed-minded person who cuts himself or herself off from discovering every dimension of truth. This is indeed the case when God's revelation is not even considered as a possibility.

> *Deprived of what Revelation offers, reason has taken side-tracks which expose it to the danger of losing sight of its final goal. Deprived of reason, faith has stressed feeling and experience, and so run the risk of no longer being a universal proposition. It is an illusion to think that faith, tied to weak reasoning, might be more penetrating; on the contrary, faith then runs the grave risk of withering into myth or superstition. By the same token, reason which is unrelated to an adult faith is not prompted to turn its gaze to the newness and radicality of being.* [12]

I think the ultimate reason for responding to God's invitation is to be happy, not only in heaven, but in this world as well. This is at the core of finding true meaning and the significance of being. If we spend our lives looking for happiness, we should just give up now and go the way of Sartre's despair and Nietzsche's insanity. In my estimation it is a futile task. If, on the other hand, we spend our lives striving to make others happy, we will in fact discover how happy we truly are! The key, I believe, is that God has made us to be people of charity and not merely consumers of gifts. The greatest joy is in the giving, not in the receiving. Any person who is honest will agree with this. When love takes hold, the joy is most profound in serving the other. This is the way we are made; and Heaven will be the experience of the perfection of our true nature.

---

12 *Fides et Ratio*, n. 48.

Faith is at the core of our life. Everybody has faith in something. Faith is what is at the heart of how we live our lives. Faith is much different than belief. If one can grant me for the sake of argument that the devil is real, then to illustrate my point, I would suggest that the devil believes in God, but has absolutely no faith in Him. The devil has faith in himself. Satan is the sole arbiter of any action he takes. As Dante recounts the devil was "tempted" to repent but uttered instead, "I will not serve!" Therefore since in our way of understanding things, Satan was outside of time and therefore made an eternal decision. Satan rejected God's love. God knows that love can only be freely given and received. God will not impose Himself on anyone, so those who refuse His love find themselves apart from God, in other words they find themselves in hell.

It is clear that Jesus was a historical figure. If there are people who seriously doubt the existence of Jesus we would have to place them in the people who would doubt the spherical nature of the earth. One can question the Divinity of Jesus, e.g. the author of the DaVinci Code, and without faith that conclusion is more understandable. Questioning something is altogether different than denying it. Facts do not depend on our ability to grasp them. Because of the eyewitness testimony of the resurrection and the host of witnesses that were willing to even forfeit their lives because of their faith in Him, it seems that one can reasonably make the decision to not only believe in Jesus, but actually put faith in Him and His Divinity. I believe there is a certain leap of faith here, but certainly not an unreasonable one.

Jesus Christ would never have us kill for the faith, but He may invite us to die for it. There have been sad moments in the Christian tradition where individuals did seem to "kill" for the faith. There likely were those who may have been led to believe that killing a moor was some kind of a good thing, but even then, only could one resort to deadly force if the person was an unjust aggressor. We need to look no farther then Calvin's Geneva to see the sad tale acted out on the non-Catholic side of Christianity. When one links religion as a means to achieve political ends one will always find disaster. With that said I do not mean to imply that religion has no part in public policy. On the contrary, the principals that respect religious liberty must be a part of every society. People must be able to practice their faith, so long as their particular faith does not threaten the life of innocent people. Faith is only dangerous when it finds itself directed towards that which is not true. The secular world seems to get it wrong on many counts, their faith in their own ideas is doomed for failure and ultimately for self-destruction. Evil is bent on its own destruction.

In all religions there is a faith dimension. All religion aims at union with the other on some level. Perfect fulfillment is the ultimate destiny that awaits us all, but where do we go from here? As I begin with a reflection on the priesthood, I feel it is important to reflect on salvation history from a Judeo-Christian perspective in particular. Hang on - here we go!

CHAPTER II · SALVATION HISTORY

One could obviously write volumes on this topic, but I also believe that it can be summarized in a way that makes a lot of sense. There is great difficulty when we try and reflect on such a topic. It is only natural to ask the question "who can we trust, or whose version of history is truly accurate?" It is difficult to know what or who to believe. Anyone can say anything they want, and truth is often believed to be nothing more than an opinion. The blogosphere is a perfect example of this. If one is willing to do the hard work of research, I do believe a person can draw some reasonable conclusions. It is also helpful to be aware of our own implicit biases, but nonetheless, I think it is very fruitful to take an objective look at things to the best of our ability.

An interesting comparison would be H.G. Wells, The Outline of History and G.K. Chesterton's account, The Everlasting Man, two vastly different accounts starting from two vastly different presuppositions, but oddly interpreting the same "data set" in vastly different ways. It seems that both want to prove what they want to believe the truth to be. I would suggest that they both cannot be correct. I also would suggest that Chesterton's approach is seemingly more rigorously scientific, which is quite ironic considering their respective conclusions.

I want to avoid the fundamentalist's argument about the world beginning about 5 or 6 thousand years ago. I would suggest that that question is not as important as others. From a Catholic perspective, the question, "How did God create the world?" is not nearly as important as embracing in faith and recognizing "*That* God created the world, and He created it out of nothing, *ex nihilo.*"

It doesn't take a rocket scientist to do a careful reading of the first two chapters of Genesis, and recognize that there are two very different stories concerning the origin of Man. Josephus, the first century historian (Jewish or Roman depending on who seemed to have the upper hand at the time), states that the first chapter of Genesis was a "philosophical " account.[13] Many of these ancient authors were much more sophisticated than many contemporaries seem to think. There is, however, something profoundly evident in these accounts, namely that God is the agent that brings creation about. It is God who says, "let there be light, and there is light." It is God who fashions Adam from the earth. A unique aspect in these creation accounts is that Man comes from God and not some primordial chaos, or some set of mythical gods who assign the fate of humanity and its members. There are no "mythical" creatures in these accounts.

Many contemporary scholars are enthralled with the concept of *myth*. Myth cannot be merely understood as a fairy tale, or a fable with a moral. They see it as pointing to primordial truths. I am quite disappointed in the lack of breadth that some scholars seem to have when reflecting on the significant differences in the Judeo-Christian creation accounts and many other creation "myths". I do not think the word myth is helpful in describing the biblical narrative. I think it more accurate to consider the creation account as a historical etiology . In other words, not a video camera portrayal of *how* God created the world, but rather a story rooted in truth, which conveys fundamental aspects of the origin of the world.

The Judeo-Christian religion has its roots in human history. No other world religion can seemingly make this claim. The Hindu religion evolved from a reflection on the Vedas, the sentences, sometimes attributed to an author or authors contemporary with the time of Abraham around 1400 to 2000 BC. Buddha growing out of the Hindu tradition was a man who sought enlightenment, and seemingly believed in his own way to have achieved it about 400 years before Jesus walked the earth. Islam began some 600 years after the

13 Jewish Antiquities, Josephus.

birth of Christ and would claim its ultimate roots through Abraham who was following the God who created Adam and Eve as the creation account relates.

It is from the perspective of the Scriptures that I hope to reflect on God's plan for the human person. There are certainly many ways to look at things. I have found a video series and study guide[14] put together by Scott Hahn and Jeff Cavins fruitful in this reflection and it certainly offers, what I would consider to be, some compelling insights. In a general sort of way, I think it may be helpful to follow loosely the organizational structure that they relate in the following reflection.

What is salvation?

Salvation is eternal survival. It means that we would live forever in security and peace with God. A Catholic hopes in one's salvation. (See Romans 8:24) As Catholics, we do not presume our salvation, and we believe that this is truly what the Bible teaches. The references here describe how Catholics understand salvation in terms of hope and not presuming salvation as merely the result of some personal proclamation of faith. Ironically the fundamentalist Christian position is in harmony with the dominant philosophical mind set that sees reality as merely perception, namely I *think* I am saved, therefore I *am* saved! Salvation is no longer a gift from God, but rather a gift as a result from *our* ability to mentally ascent to a concept.

One of my relatives asked me to meet with her and her boyfriend who was a serious Christian, but believed that Catholics are woefully misguided. He was a very dedicated man and I am convinced that he had a passionate faith. I can remember the evening. I was still a seminarian, and we met at a local Mexican chain restaurant. Normally I would have had a Margarita, but I felt that might just reinforce some negative Catholic stereotypes. We had a wonderful discussion sharing why we thought we were both correct, throwing bible verses back and forth and not making much headway. As I recall the conversation began to revolve around philosophy and how Paul said to reject the worldly philosophies. I was quick to agree, but I felt he didn't really

---

14 Our Father's Plan, Cavins, Jeff, and Hahn, Scott, Ignatius Press, San Francisco, 2002.

get what St. Paul was trying to convey. I really could see that this man was a good man, so I politely asked him, "Do you mind if I am a little blunt?" He graciously accepted my invitation.

I proceeded to give him a thumbnail sketch of the development of the western mind that went something like this. For the Greeks truth was transcendent. In fact the very word they use implies uncovering the object or thing under investigation. They believed that the world was eternal and basically this concept has been the root of modern physics and its first law, namely that matter can neither be created nor destroyed. Christian revelation accepted much of the ancient Greek's recognition of the transcendent, but biblical revelation informed the Christians that matter was in fact created. Things were humming right along to the time of Descartes who posited, *"cogito ergo sum"*, *I think therefore I am*. Basically he recognized that as much as he tried to clear his mind, the rational concepts remained, hence he was a rational being. Unfortunately, philosophy seemed to go down hill from there for about 400 years. Most seem to embrace the concept *"I think therefore it is!"*. In other words the human person's idea is what makes truth what it is. So I asked him, "what sounds more like the worldly philosophy of the day, "I hope in my salvation because God can save even me!" or "I think I am saved, so therefore I am!" He started to cry. He realized, so it would seem, that he had embraced the same kind of thinking that does so much damage to individuals in our world today.

The Catholic understanding of salvation is more nuanced and rooted in a broader reading of the Scriptures. Paul notes that we are saved by hope, and hope is confident assurance of the things not yet seen. Consider the following verses.

> **Romans 8:24** *For in this hope we were saved. Now hope that is seen is not hope. For who hopes for what he sees?*
>
> **Psalm 19:13** *From presumption restrain your servant and let it not rule me. Then I shall be blameless, clean from grave sin.*[15]

---

15 The Abbey Psalter, the Book of Psalms used by the Trappist monks of Genesee Abbey, Paulist Press, 1981, excerpt from Psalm 19.

Also St. Paul would point to the fact that salvation can be lost, we must respond to God's offer of salvation by our response to His grace:

> **1 Corinthians 9:23 - 10:4** *I do it all for the sake of the gospel, that I may share in its blessings. Do you not know that in a race all the runners compete, but only one receives the prize? So run that you may obtain it. Every athlete exercises self-control in all things. They do it to receive a perishable wreath, but we an imperishable.* ***Well, I do not run aimlessly, I do not box as one beating the air; but I pommel my body and subdue it, lest after preaching to others I myself should be disqualified.*** *I want you to know, brethren, that our fathers were all under the cloud, and all passed through the sea, and all were baptized into Moses in the cloud and in the sea, and all ate the same supernatural food and all drank the same supernatural drink. For they drank from the supernatural Rock which followed them, and the Rock was Christ.[NAB]*

Sadly the extreme fundamentalist view, once saved - always saved, is ironically rooted in the contemporary worldly philosophy that limits truth to one's own perception. This concept virtually plagues the contemporary mind and contributes to the way most people function from day to day. It would be logically dismissed if put in the proper context by thinking adults. For example many people dismiss universal absolutes us unrealistic or out of the question, but if a person believes something to be true it is true for them. (e.g. I think abortion is ok, therefore it is ok for me) Sadly many have fallen prey to this worldly philosophy by embracing the thought, "I think I am saved, therefore I am!" God can save who ever He wants to save. God can save the followers of Mohammad, the Buddhists, the Hindus, and all people of good will. As Catholics we hope in our salvation and humbly submit to a merciful and loving God.

Democracy is valued, but it must never be absolute. If most people thought rape to be acceptable, would that make it so? Many would say that is a ridiculous example, but it wasn't too many years ago, when most people thought slavery was just fine! I can remember a person giving a speech once said, "We must never have the right to do what is wrong!" Again it comes back to common sense and the ability to make the effort to uncover the truth as it is, and not merely as we would like it to be. Truth is discernable: people know that murder is wrong!

Salvation is revealed to us in human history and this is one way to see how it all works towards God's plan for us. I realize that history certainly reveals God, if there is a God to reveal, but looking at the religious milieu as we find it, there does seem to be one religion that is more discernable as it relates to history as we know it. It would be hard to argue against the premise that the historical God is the God of the Jews. It is their story that has led and continues to lead me on my faith journey.

Pre - History

There is a time that relates to an era before recorded history. There are many accounts from various cultures that try and make sense out of the human experience and the origins of the human person. The Bible gives us what Karl Rahner[16] would call a historical etiology. In other words it would be an account that is rooted in history. This story of creation is not intended to be a video camera type portrayal of the events. The Genesis account shows us that God creates out of nothing, *ex nihilo*. Unlike the faith assumption for science, "matter can neither be created nor destroyed", it is God who takes this pride of place, and it is He who creates all things, matter included, and ultimately it is He who can neither be created nor destroyed.. The act of faith is somewhat analogous, to that which true faith is directed. For the agnostic it is matter that is eternal, for the believer it is God that is eternal. Is it matter that is eternal, or is it God? The Jews, Christians and Muslims all recognize that it is God who is eternal.

The lesson from the Genesis accounts is that God creates out of nothing. Out of the formless void, God creates order, and then fills it with His creation, His beings, and His "*creatures*". Man is His crowning glory and God ultimately enters into a covenant with Man. The covenant is an essential concept for us to grasp. A covenant is much more than merely a contract. It is an agreement rooted in love. It also implies a relationship rooted in love. Salvation history is loaded with covenants,

---

16 Karl Rahner was a prominent theologian who contributed much to the reforms of the Second Vatican Council and contemporary theological reflection.

and drawing from reflections by Scott Hahn, it is interesting to note how salvation history can be centered on seven covenants that take place at various stages in salvation history. Six covenants have come to pass, and we await the seventh when Christ will return in the fullness of His glory. At the very least this is a very interesting way to look at salvation history.

The Covenant between Adam and Eve

God reveals to man the marriage covenant. Adam, while not satisfied with all the animals that God created, finally recognizes in Eve the singular gift of that relationship. John Paul II in his reflections on the Theology of the Body[17] notes how this relationship points to the deep center of which man truly is meant to be. Namely Man and Woman, united as one, reflect, in a very profound way, the mystery of God Himself in the Trinity. This first covenant includes two people. It is in this relationship that man can pierce the "original solitude" that is reflected in the Genesis account.

The Covenant between Noah's Family and God

Next the covenant broadens to include a whole family, Noah and his sons and their wives. While the world lost its way, God established a covenant that extended to several families.

The Covenant with Abraham

According to Scott Hahn, some scholars speculate that Shem, one of Noah's sons, also the one who is seen as the father of the "Semite" line, was the link between the pre-historic accounts and the more historical accounts beginning with Abraham. This link is found in the priest Melchizadek. If one follows the "narrative history"[18] in Genesis, Shem

---

17 The Theology of the Body, Pauline Books and Media, a compilation of the 129 papal audiences from early on in John Paul II's pontifical ministry.

18 Narrative history is intended to relate to the "story" that is told. It is quite possible that the authors of the text were not intending to relate a "literal" history, but related the details in such a way that would have a meaningful significance to Jewish history. It would be a story rooted in truth, but specific dates may not be perfectly accurate.

lives to the time of Abraham. Shem, in the minds of some, is identified with the character Melchizadek. Melchizadek was the priest who offered bread and wine and was also the king of Salem or ancient Jerusalem. It is noteworthy that the Covenant is now extended to include an entire tribe.

The Covenant with Moses

After the people are delivered from the oppressive slavery of pharaoh and the Egyptians, the covenant is established with the entire nation. This was manifested ultimately in temple worship and was centered around the Ark of the Covenant. The Ark contained the tablets of the Ten Commandments, the staff of Aaron, and a cup of the Manna that sustained the Israelites in their 40 years in the desert. The 40 years was God's way of honoring Moses' plea to be merciful after the people rejected God's plan for them to take possession of the land He had prepared for them. Now the covenant has been extended to the 12 tribes of Israel, an entire nation.

The Covenant with David

David rises to power and God enters into His everlasting covenant with David. Now the covenant extends not only to a single nation or tribal grouping, but an entire kingdom. Many nations are united under the kingship of David. At this time in history Israel has risen to the status of a world power. The covenant is made with many nations. Sadly it will soon be divided as the result of David's infidelity and sin.

The Coming of Christ

Christ comes to heal the divided kingdom as the long awaited messiah, but does more than that. The new and everlasting covenant extends to the entire earth. Not only is the kingdom united, but all the kingdoms and nations of the world are drawn and called to be one in Christ, who is the light to all nations.

This is obviously merely a thumbnail sketch of humanity's destiny. I am often incredulous over this seemingly unspectacular people and how they rose to power some 3000 years ago. What I find most intriguing about their story is their brutal honesty. Their heroes often have tarnished reputations and are not perfect by any stretch of the imagination. Their history is marred by those who broke faith, and also those who were gloriously steadfast. They call those faithful ones, the poor ones or the little ones, or in Hebrew the *anawim* (on-a-weem). All people in their own personal faith journey will have to face the question as to which side one falls, upon the *little ones* or those "who have ears but do not hear, or have eyes but do not see!"

CHAPTER III · THE PRIESTHOOD IN THE ROMAN CATHOLIC CHURCH

First off, the priesthood is a complex reality in the Roman Catholic Church. It is indeed a ministry of presence, service and fatherhood. Contrary to popular belief, there are Catholic priests who love the Church, believe in her teachings and are in communion with the pope who are in fact married! They even revere the teaching of celibacy! These might be Episcopalian priests who, though not originally Roman Catholic, made the choice to live out their Christian faith in the Roman Catholic Tradition. These men were accepted to be ordained priests for the Church. They came to believe that the tradition that they had served departed from the biblical and apostolic teachings of Jesus. Likely the principals that may have contributed to their move might include recent decisions that changed their practice concerning the ordination of women and failing to recognize difficulties with those engaged in the active homosexual lifestyle serving as ordained ministers. These issues will be more thoroughly discussed later, but suffice to say that these issues and how they are viewed result from the way people view the bible and the ability to know truth itself.

There would also be my brother priests in the Eastern Rites who had been married before being ordained and have chosen to be priests. These clearly are the exceptions and not the rule, but nonetheless this is the reality. My point is simply that marriage is not some kind of impediment to the essence of the priesthood. In pope Benedict's document on the Eucharist, *Sacramentum Caritatis,* he emphasizes that celibacy is not something that should be seen first as something to make someone more available for service, on the contrary, it is to make one more focused on God and look more directly towards God for all your needs.

Family life and marriage when lived faithfully takes heroic sacrifice, family members are made extremely available for the immediate needs of those around them. I sometimes am in awe over the beautiful and profound sacrifices that husbands and wives make for each other and their families. Obviously this is not the case in all families. Likewise many priests squander the gift of celibacy by freeing themselves from family obligations and hence direct there energies in things that are not particularly spiritual. All vocations are directed as serving God and the human person, the celibate vocation is to put a certain primacy on serving others through their more immediate service to God, while those who pursue secular vocations are called to serve God through their more immediate service to others.

In society many fail to appreciate the significance and distinctiveness of fatherhood. Only women can be mothers and only men can be fathers. God is more than just a Father and more than just a Mother. To live one's vocation fully is to deeply reveal God's real presence in the world.

The priest is to radiate fatherhood. The priest is to reflect as fully as possible those dimensions of the divine which are the true source of all that is good. The priest needs to give without counting the cost. Any good, natural father makes all kinds of sacrifices for his family. So too, the priest must be selfless in his dedication to the people entrusted to his care. A father cannot live the lives of his children any more than a priest can live the lives of his spiritual flock. A good father will take time to instruct his children on how to live well. God has instructed us through His prophets and His Divine revelation. God was selfless in His sacrifice for His people and He invites His priests to do the same.

Many seem to suggest that celibacy was an invention of the middle ages. If one has any sense of history at all, this position borders on the absurd, it is a very untenable position. I find it quite interesting when someone comes up and suggests that only men are priests because the church was conditioned by the historical time period. While this may seem to be a plausible position, it seems somewhat unlikely. If one honestly takes a look at the early historical period, one would be hard pressed to draw such conclusions. In the early years, as the Church was becoming more structured and after the destruction of the temple in or around 67 AD, the Christians were forced to distance themselves from the Jewish faith. The early Christians took many things from the pagan religions, particularly feast days, Christmas for example. It would seem, in order to further define themselves, it would have been more logical if the early Christians would have adopted the then current and normative pagan practices of priestesses. But they did not. The only evidence that I am aware of concerning priestesses would be a reference to Thecla, likely a mythical companion of Paul who was instructed to preach and teach and baptize. Thecla was seemingly created by an early Asiatic Presbyter, this according to Tertullian, a contemporary author of the time who testifies to its fictional origin.[19] Some others point to the reference of Aquila in the bible, but the reference is not the celebration of the liturgy or the mass but an "agape" meal about which Paul cautioned some people from abusing the practice. I sometimes wonder if this is the passage others may misinterpret to only celebrate the Eucharist infrequently.

The sad reality of many of the contemporary arguments against the teachings and practice of the Church is that they are not rooted in the historical development of God's plan for His people. Instead of honestly trying to reflect on the tradition and God's plan, people seem quick to dismiss the history as antiquated or even useless in deepening our understanding of the world. The Church believes that it has developed under the guidance of the Holy Spirit and that which is best for the human person's natural

19 Ante-Nicene Fathers, Vol. 8, ed. Roberts, Alexander, D.D. and Donaldson, James, LL.D., Hendrickson Publishers, 2nd printing, 1995, p. 355.

fulfillment is at the heart of her teachings. Many seem to call into question God's plan and that He ultimately has the human person's best interest at heart.

First I would simply like to point to the tradition and the development of the priesthood today. This topic in itself is worthy of a book. I would suggest Christian Cochini's, <u>The Apostolic Origins of Priestly Celibacy</u>[20] and more recently <u>The Case for Clerical Celibacy</u>: <u>*Its Historical Development and Theological Foundations*</u> [21] for a thorough treatment of the topic. More directly one can look to the basic biblical references in Paul's letters and the Matthew's Gospel as well. Often times people will look to Paul and dismiss his so called "sexist attitudes", but in the nineteenth chapter of Matthew, Jesus Himself seems to address the topic. It also is worthy of placing the subject in the context in which we find it. Jesus is teaching on the intended purpose of marriage, a topic that we will indeed address more fully. Suffice it to say, Jesus lays out God's intention of marriage between a man and a woman, so that the two may become one flesh. Jesus clearly states that marriage, as a permanent and unbreakable bond, was His Father's intention from the beginning. He is trying to resolve the dispute that the Pharisees and lawyers have raised to trap Him. He points to the fact that divorce was allowed because of the hardness of the peoples hearts. The demand of such a relationship is evident, and His apostles, those who would become the primary leaders and teachers of the Church, in fact raise the question of marriage. If marriage is to have such a priority and not merely something to add pleasure and diversion to one's life, then the apostles suggest that it is better not to marry! Jesus bluntly agrees but with the caveat, "Not all can accept this, but only those to whom it has been given!" Jesus sets the stage for what the Catholic Church would later see as annulments[22] or marriages that resulted from

20 Christian Cochini (Paperback) - October 1990.

21 Alphonso M. Stickler, Alfons Maria Cardinal Stickler (Paperback), Ignatius Press

22 This is a recognition that a ***sacramental*** marriage never existed from the beginning. The church makes no judgment on the legitimacy of the children

porneia, the Greek word which likely suggests an unlawful marriage, as well as the benefits of remaining single for the kingdom of God. Jesus states that it is better not to marry if one is to be a leader in the Church. However he does not exclude the possibility. He just seems to see it as the exception as opposed to that which is normative (in other words, what the Catholic Church teaches and has taught since biblical times).

As early as the council of Elvira[23]in the early fourth century there were rules concerning apostolic celibacy. It is unfortunate that many who consider themselves to be academic elites demonstrate such ignorance in this matter. It is often argued that priestly celibacy is an invention of the middle ages. This is sheer nonsense. It may have not been the universal discipline, but it was a practice from the earliest times. The contemporary adage seems to apply: "repeat a lie often enough and people will begin to believe it."

Let us turn to some potentially rather politically incorrect ways of thinking. It does not take a rocket scientist or a biologist to recognize that men and women are different creatures. Any mature adult who has come from a somewhat functional family with healthy human relations begins to realize there is something quite different about the opposite sex. The differences should not be viewed as better or worse, but certainly different. When one begins to apply science to the differences they become even more evident. Emotionally and physically men and women are quite different. One of the physiological differences that I find quite fascinating is the place in the brain where emotions are processed in the respective sexes. In a woman, this region of the brain is the size of about a silver dollar, in a man, the size of a dime! No surprise here! Women, generally speaking, seem to be naturally inclined to have the ability to process emotions a lot more efficiently than men. Conversely men are perennially less sensitive then women as a general rule. On the other hand, men, generally speaking, are more physically powerful than women. Therefore, if there is intelligent design, e.g. God making

---

sired, or the legality of the civil bond. It makes a judgment concerning the free and uncoerced intent of both the man and women at the time vows were exchanged.

23 http://www.newadvent.org/cathen/05395b.htm

stuff, it seems to be logical that if there is an attack that threatens, the man will not be able to process the debilitating emotions such as fear as efficiently as women. This helps men to be less susceptible to fear or other emotions that would tend to lessen there ability to fend off attackers. Men are equipped to be better defenders, while women naturally are more sensitive and naturally more nurturing. One need not look very far to see the down side of such insensitivity in men. An aspect of the priest's ministry is to be empathetic, but also strong. It is important for the priest to be sensitive to the emotions while not letting the emotions overly impact a decision he may be compelled to make.

Debates rage in our society regarding the priesthood. It seems evident that the issue of women priests has been resolved in the Catholic Church to the chagrin of many. Not only was the document, *Ordinatio Sarcerdotalis*[24] promulgated in 1994 but this was followed by the subsequent *Dubium* (an official question submitted to Rome for clarification) that clearly, and I would argue infallibly, set forth the position that the Church has no authority to make such a change that would ordain women. I really think that God wants us to be as happy as we can possibly be. I am convinced that people will sometimes do things not because they feel it is God's will, but because they have been duped by the ideologies of others. Sadly, this will lead to their own sense of being oppressed and often at the expense of their own personal happiness.

A priest is a father, a man of God, who has been called by God and God's Church to make present in a sacramental way the presence of God working and living among us in a very external way. Henri DeLubac states this distinction quite well in his book, The Splendor of the Church[25]. It is interesting to note that I believe he wrote this book while under censure by the Church that he was defending. In his book he makes a very meaningful distinction between what he calls the *external* and *internal* dimension of the priesthood. Through baptism we all share in the "internal" manifestation of Christ's priesthood, while the ministerial priesthood is a more "external"

---

24 The Vatican Website

25 The Splendor of the Church, De Lubac, Henri, Ignatius Press, 384 pages.

manifestation of Christ's priesthood. Historically, Jesus Christ was a man and so on some objective level, it is easier for the human being to connect with the reality of Christ in His historical manifestation as a man. I suspect the previous lines made the blood pressure rise in many who read them. I suspect they may have even caused an expletive or two to be muttered under one's breath, or maybe even out loud, but I think it is important to reflect on whether there is any truth in what was said. We must honestly and objectively ponder it in our hearts.

Before the early nineties, I entertained the question regarding women priests as an open one theologically. When I was a student in engineering at Purdue I attended a lecture sponsored by the Newman center at the parish. The title of the presentation as I recall was, "Sexism in the Catholic Church". I came with no agenda; in fact I thought how difficult it must be for a woman who felt she was called to be a priest. As I listened I could hardly believe what I was hearing. This woman was a religious sister who had a PhD and went on nothing less than a tirade. She angrily attempted to build a case on why women needed to be priests. She felt that this was important because women needed the power! Eek! This is the wrong reason to be a priest, and if any men want to be priests for such reasons they should not be allowed to pursue the vocation of the priesthood. She then claimed that the Church systematically oppressed women and never allowed them to share their thoughts or writings. After her presentation I challenged her allegations in a loving and charitable way, I thought. I asked her about a woman who wrote in the late Middle Ages, Mary of Agreda. This particular work deepened my own spirituality and insight into the demands of the Gospel. She looked at me seemingly scornfully and dismissed my observation. She was just flatly wrong in her analysis. Was her education so narrow as to have missed Theresa of Avilla or the great effect Catherine of Sienna had on the Pope and his return to Rome for Avignon? Even in the Old Testament one can see that the Judeo-Christian ethic saw woman as much more then merely property. Again, people can say whatever they want, but history tells a different tale. Certainly there were abuses, but the Church among the cultures of the world saw women as equal in that hope for salvation. This encounter was before the Church had spoken so definitively on the matter of women priests. I felt that it would not have, in the least bit, shaken my faith had the Church made the contrary judgment regarding women priests, but with that said, I think the issue has been resolved. In fact, I think the decision was made to protect women and help them to realize their value and their mission as a true mother, in religious life or in the married state. This role is quite different from being a father or a priest. Only a woman can be a mother, and only a man can be a father.

The apostles were able to recognize the demands of the ministry. They seemed to realize that a person could be freer to serve others if that person was not married. This is just clearly the truth. In fact, I know of protestant ministers who admitted or saw the benefit of being not married for the kingdom of God. In my own life I truly felt I could never give my wife all the attention that she would deserve and still serve God in the way that I perceived Him to be calling me. This is not a negative judgment on marriage. On the contrary, it is a brutally honest recognition of its true demands and my own personal limitations. If a person lives marriage as a true sacrament they will agree with what I am saying. In the Catholic Church, marriage is not only seen as something good or even great, it is seen as something Holy! Many in the world fail to recognize the great dignity and value of the institution of marriage in the human family.

I was asked to give a talk to a neighboring protestant church on the common things that we share. It was a great evening and at the end of the presentation, I opened the floor to questions. A woman brought up the celibacy question, and I responded in much the same way as I did above. I related the demands of service and how difficult it would be on any woman who had to deal with the competing demands of the priest's own family commitments and the demands of his parish family. I then said, it would not be impossible, but I honestly think the woman would have to be a living saint. At that the crowd began to laugh. It was the pastor's wife who raised the question. The veracity of the explanation seemed self-evident.

A priest, above all, is one who is called to be a father, one who helps people value life: their own life and the lives of others. This is at the heart of the mission of the priest. I will be so bold as to say than any priest who fails in this dimension of his priesthood has failed to understand its essence. God made life and it was good. The priest must be the person who will defend all people's right to life, especially the most vulnerable. The reason is simple: all people have the potential to bring Christ to the world and be His living presence in the world. The essence of fatherhood is to be a life giver, a defender, and indeed a lover of all that is good.

A father on every level truly plants the seed. He must be the one who brings those natural gifts to fruition. The priest cannot be a mother, but he must be a father. He must reflect those attributes of strength and justice. He must be willing to do the right thing even when misunderstood or misjudged.

No one is perfect, so it is important to rely on prayer and right judgment. Any good father will always listen to his children and draw from their insight. At the same time he must follow the wisdom that he has accrued through his own lived experience and his own family. The Church is the family of Man. No person on earth is without a father. Many have suffered at the hands of their physical father, and some have suffered as the result of priests who have betrayed their vows, but God has provided for His world through the Church the gift of real fatherhood. My prayer for all, especially those who have been deprived of a good father, is that they may discover this real treasure of fatherhood in the family of the Church.

Chapter IV · The World, Its gods, Its Illusions and Its Faith

The World

I am not anxious to set up a huge dichotomy between the world of God and the world of the Human person. There are excellent people in our world and there are some in my estimation that are woefully misguided. I hope to provide some insight, or at least some perspectives that may assist some people in deepening their reflections on this world and its true purpose. On the brighter side I see Bill Bennett's work on the virtues as a great contribution to the good in our world[26] On the darker side, the world in its pejorative sense is well represented by other works that are less inspiring such as Papal Sin, and Why I am a Catholic by Garry Wills. One could certainly include a recent popular novel, The DaVinci Code by Dan Brown, which purports to be fiction, but however it uses real organizations within the Church and caricatures its mission and its members as blind fanatics bent on keeping the real "truth" from the world.

Some contemporary authors epitomize the world and its illusions. An important distinction to keep in mind is the fundamental approach with which people think. I would suggest that sometimes, through no culpable fault of their own, (I hope) people have failed to realize

26 The Book of Virtues, and The Moral Compass, Simon and Schuster, Rockefeller Center, 1230 Avenue of the Americas, New York, NY 10020, 1995.

that basic decisions are quite simple. Mr. Wills, for example, makes the charge that some contemporary doctrinal arguments are "so intellectually contemptible that mere self respect forbids a man to voice them as his own".[27] It seems to be an impossibility, according to Mr. Wills, for a Catholic who believes in the teachings of the Church, such as recognizing artificial contraception as an offense against humanity, the current discipline of Clerical Celibacy, and the seemingly non-reformable doctrine of admitting women to the ministerial priesthood, to be anything other than some kind of a mental midget or to be simply intellectually dishonest. I can see how he could be correct if a person subscribes to the philosophical framework that admits to the impossibility of knowing the truth. In other words, if one embraces the self-contradictory position that there are no absolutes, except of course for the *absolute* that there are no absolutes, then and seemingly only then is Mr. Wills' assessment plausible. The sad irony in such a position is tragic, but at the same time it is assumed to be the "truth" in the minds of most people.

Absolutes are by no means common in my own estimation, but I posit they do exist. To use an outlandish example, I would suggest that it is absolutely wrong without exception to put a cigarette butt out in a child's eye! Another absolute that I have affirmed by faith is that I have taken for granted in this work that Jesus is the Son of the Living God. I grant that I may be mistaken, but the fact remains that either Jesus Christ is God, or He is not. I feel compelled to accept the principle of non-contradiction. After all, science is a respectable discipline, and reality is predictable, if even perceived by some as chaotic. It would seem, according to most people's experience that the only thing that can ultimately care for the world or destroy it is the human person. There are natural disasters, but most seem to believe that the human person is the greatest threat to the world and its future. It is for this reason that there are so many debates that rage wildly from global warming to endangered species, to the most pointed and perilous questions relating to weapons of mass destruction. And yet, from a purely scientific world view, man is the world's only hope for enduring. It would seem, by the best scientific estimates that we have plenty of time to develop technologies that could even

27 Papal Sin, p. 5.

44

reach another star by the time this one wears out. Unfortunately many people it seems are more concerned about earthly pleasure, possessions and power than to work towards more noble goals such as reaching for the stars, or feeding the hungry, or developing the arts which all ultimately stem from knowing, appreciating and marveling at the beauty and intrinsic dignity of the human person. Those who find themselves in positions of power want to impose upon the masses a dictatorship of relativism. Pope Benedict XVI warns of such a position. Ultimately such a position allows one person to be "relatively" more important than another, and thus feeds war, strife and discontent throughout the world.

Honestly, humanity has a very poor track record, especially when it looks to itself for guidance. Past societies are merely a litany of various quests for power, domination and control. In recent history one need only look at the debacles of Fascism, Nazism, and Communism as examples of systems built on human understanding alone. Regimes seem to ultimately collapse as a result of their respective failure to understand the workings of the human person. You can only oppress some group for so long until they revolt. What if we could come to realize that the human person is not the ultimate enemy of the human person? I would argue that ignorance is a powerful enemy of the human person. Ignorance stems from a lack of true insight, and ignorance is simply evil. Literally, ignorance is a privation of knowledge or lacking insight into things as they are. I suggest that humanity is well served by relying on the philosophical tradition that evil is a lack; it is nothingness, a privation. This can serve to be profoundly helpful as we reflect on humanity's hope. I also believe it to be simply true!

I think it is fairly safe to begin with the scientific premise (science's faith presupposition) that matter can never be created nor destroyed. Sadly it seems that the world is unwilling to even base its behavior on such a basic premise. The "world" has seemed to reject this and wants to say, "I can create things in my mind, or my understanding". The world has reduced its god to merely one of personal perception. It would seem that if a person comes to believe something that becomes something that cannot be called into question, even at the expense of the personal human dignity of others.

45

Human dignity is at the heart of all that the Church teaches. I mentioned in the earlier chapter how I begin my ethics class. It is a simple way to help the students realize how important they are as human beings. We as humans are infinitely valuable and no one has the right to tell a person what to believe or what to think, but we really do have an obligation to help others recognize what is true and good. If one values human dignity then everything the Catholic Church professes in her ethical teaching makes sense: from its prohibition on Artificial Contraception, or the huge distinction between embryonic stem cell research and the permitted adult stem cell research, to its prohibition of abortion or Euthanasia.

Time and again the world has failed to recognize human dignity. This is evident by its promotion of human slavery in the past to its current eugenic policies, policies which seems to see abortion as a kind of sacrament. Also, there is the degrading way secular society seems to view human sexual relations as nothing more than recreation or a mode of experiencing pleasure. Bishop Robert Finn of the Diocese of Kansas City published a pastoral letter in Lent of 2007 which addresses pornography. It summarizes the massive problem of pornography and its impact.[28] Society's wrongheaded view of human sexuality assaults families and contributes to oppression and sexual exploitation.

The Real World is a place of order. It makes sense, but our ability to understand the mechanisms of the world are quite limited. The philosophical premise that truth is merely dependant on one's perception seems to have found its way even into the understanding of theoretical physics. Even the work of Steven Hawkings, the world renowned physicist, on quantum mechanics seems to run counter, or not obviously reconcilable with another rather gifted intellectual, Albert Einstein, his quote is telling:[29]

> *Quantum mechanics is very impressive. But an inner voice tells me that it is not yet the real thing. The theory yields a lot,*

---

28 *Blessed are the Pure of Heart: A Pastoral Letter on the Dignity of the Human Person and the Dangers of Pornography*, Bishop Robert Finn, Chancery Office, 300 E. 36th St., P.O. Box 419037, Kansas City, MO 64141-6037, February 21, 2007.

29 --Albert Einstein from http://home.att.net/~quotations/einstein.html

*but it hardly brings us any closer to the secret of the Old One.
In any case I am convinced that He doesn't play dice.*

There is another interesting story about Albert Einstein. The story is told of a young priest near Princeton, who had just been ordained and wanted to meet Mr. Einstein. He went to where he lived and explained the he was just ordained to the priesthood and Mr. Einstein was gracious enough to receive him. He showed great interest in the priest. Mr. Einstein seemed almost anxious for the young priest to tell him more about the Eucharist. I wonder what would have happened had that young priest continued the dialogue with Mr. Einstein.[30]

H.G. Wells wrote, The Outline of History, and proceeded to explain things from a "scientific" perspective, indeed a perspective that seems to almost deify science. G.K. Chesterton references the work often in his book, The Everlasting Man, which seems to provide a reasonable scientific critique of some of the assumptions seemingly made by Wells. For Chesterton, science is not the god, but rather a tool to more deeply penetrate the mystery of God.

Joseph Campbell also has contributed significantly to the body of literature that relates to "myth" and he seems to be a little discouraged that the contemporary person is slow to "create" some new myths that can put forth his hopes for the human person's divinity. I wonder if he has read J.R.R. Tolkien's body of literature, from The Hobbit to the Lord of the Rings Trilogy, and posthumously, The Silmarillion. This particular work is myth at it best and in what I would consider to be myth in the true sense of the word.

All this scholarly work ultimately begs the question, why do people write? Is it merely, "Publish or perish?" Is there a deep drive at sincerity and truth, or is novelty the motivation. I remember the scene in the Hollywood portrayal of the screenplay, *Murder in the Cathedral*, in the movie *Becket*, with Peter O'Toole and Richard Burton. The scene is set with Becket waiting for his audience with the pope. Some cardinals are pondering the value of sincerity as a valid tool of manipulation - the irony is amazing.

---

30 The basis of this story was related in a spiritual conference led by Benedict Groschel for the priests of the diocese of Fort Wayne-South Bend, Indiana, circa 2005.

Sincerity: it is worth reflecting on a bit. It is believed by some that the ancient roots of the word stem from "*sem*" meaning one, and *cerus* "to grow". Is it a reach to suggest that the sincere person is a person who wants to grow in oneness? Also some see its roots from the Latin which can be literally interpreted, "without wax". Is a sincere person one who seeks not division, but unity? Would it be someone who tries not to cover over things? How many people are truly sincere, especially when it comes to religion? How many truly make the measured calculation, "What is in it for me?"

One need not ask this question only about religious belief, but political tendencies, business practices, etc, etc., etc. I often wonder how many people are willing to even confront the question themselves. Sincerity at its root reveals our deepest understanding of self, our desires, our understanding, and dare I even say it, our faith. Faith is that thing that we all must have in something, whether it be oneself, or the One, Holy, Catholic and Apostolic Church. It could also be a host of things in between, e.g. Karl Marx, Sigmund Freud, Frederick Nietzsche, Buddha, Mohammad, Gandhi, or some nebulous new age concept or ideology. Ultimately I have chosen not to follow a dead guy. Jesus is risen and I have this on the testimony of many. This claim about the resurrection is a singular claim, the only one that is corroborated by significant eyewitness testimonies. It can clearly be denied, but it certainly is not unreasonable to embrace it.

I do believe that Karol Wotija (John Paul II) has truly uncovered something intrinsically significant about the heart of human anthropology. Namely that we humans all desire at least three things: pleasure, possessions and power. In the early papal audiences he uses the categories, lust of the flesh, and lust of the eyes and the pride of life. These desires are deeply ingrained in our humanity. Like the intricate components of a fine watch, it is only through an accurate understanding of the way something really works, that we can ever hope to repair it when it becomes damaged. Face it, humanity is damaged goods! Something needs fixed, and humanity's real task is to do just that, but until there is real, concrete, immutable insight into what makes us tick, we will not be very successful. Until we can fully know the truth and share it with the world, there will be members of our race willing to continue to fly jets into buildings, plot nuclear devastation, blow themselves up in throngs of innocents, and continue to exploit the poor and the undereducated and underprivileged. People will choose to place there own political advantage or personal comfort over the welfare of the common good.

In western civilization we have so much at our disposal. We are generally free societies and have so many options. I marvel at the lives that have so much of these "objective components", namely pleasure, possessions and power within their reach. I am thinking of the Hollywood elites, or those of high political office, and yet on a personal level, they typically live devastatingly tragic lives, often fraught with depression, or they live deeply "medicated" lives. It comes back to the meaning of life question, which ultimately comes back to the "truth" question. How many people lose their own life, after gaining what was perceived to be their dream? Did you ever consider how difficult it must be to walk down the street and be recognized by the vast majority of people you meet? The cost of fame is awfully high, is it not? Did you ever consider the burden one must carry if one is wealthy and has all those extra managerial burdens to carry? Quoting the popular movie, *Spider Man* and Peter Parker's guardian, "With great power, comes great responsibility".

Its gods! Humans are religious by nature and want to serve. The gods, by definition have the capacity to make things happen, they govern reality. Therefore the logic seems to be if the person gives their allegiance to the god, then the god is supposed to make "good" things happen to its adherent.

We all want to know the real truth. How many people are looking for that guru, or thing, or book or answer that will make all things right? Where can it be found? Sincerity is a tough standard, but I think it is the only valid one. I was at a small political gathering. One of my parishioners was running for a position as a state representative of the local district, and our state congressman was there lending his support. As it turns out, my cousin is civilly married to his sister, so after some small talk, I asked him the question, "Are people in Washington really sincere; do they really care?" Being the excellent politician that he is, I believe he turned it back on me and asked that about priests. I found it to be a valid point. The reality is that we ultimately can only answer that question as we look in the mirror. In this case, I believe that this particular politician is sincere. The world gets messy and compromises are made. In the end, the degree of sincerity will dictate the degree of the compromise one is willing to make. It also will determine what aspects of any issue are judged to be open to compromise. It does, however, come back to truth. The pilot who is taking off cannot make compromises with the physical limitations with the aircraft. There are certain limitations that cannot be overcome. I also suggest that if we understand the human person correctly, there are certain things that we also cannot compromise. Human dignity and the value of life are indeed at the heart of such things.

Sadly I think at the heart of the matter for most people is money. This is the most popular god that drives our society today. I certainly believe that church leaders are not free from this temptation, even Paul warned us about church leaders that are only in the ministry for personal gain. As a diocesan priest the temptations are harder to act on because of the nature of the pay scales, but sad to say, historically it sure seems like decisions have been made on financial expediency rather than on what seemed more just and right. Individuals in the Church are just that, individuals, though the Church is perfect in her teachings, individuals are far from perfect in putting them into practice.

Societies will enshrine what they value. If one beckons back to the Middle Ages and ponders what the prominent buildings in the population centers were, it would be the churches. It is likely that in the various villages the church spires would be the first to pierce the horizon. Today it is the bank buildings and the insurance companies! That is really a reflection of where our society places its ultimate hope, its *security*. I think this is a very sad commentary, but I also think it reveals something that is profoundly true. The god that seems to hold the greatest sway is money, or the biblical phrase mammon.

Its Illusions

The world and the political order is all about compromise, but if we compromise on the wrong things the results will be catastrophic. If we compromise on things that are fundamentally wrong, then it will be only a matter of time before the natural order corrects itself. It is for this reason we must do all in our power to understand clearly the human person and what will serve him or her best. We must not be driven by illusion, but rather we must strive to know the real and that which is objectively true.

The Divine Feminine

Throughout history one cannot argue against the fact that women have seemed to get the short end of the stick. Why would this be the case? Is it just because the male is physically, as a general rule, more powerful, domineering and driven by power and control? The mythical gods have a variety of forms and often reinforce such thinking. The Christian faith, however, holds to what it perceives to have been divinely revealed in the Mystery of the Trinity, a powerful, all-just God that truly transcends gender. God is neither exclusively masculine (the manifestation of the Incarnation of Jesus being a separate case) nor feminine, but has one divine nature that reveals something transcendent about God's identity. God is well beyond the masculine and feminine and yet there is something in the masculine and feminine that reveals aspects of the divine. Human marriage also presents an image of God and God's attributes. Aspects of the male and female united in the bond of marriage reflect a deep truth as is understood in the ancient Christian religion. It is fascinating to me that pagan religions saw women as nothing more than a vessel to be used, and at the same time given seemingly more credibility by many today than Christianity.

Since women have seemingly been treated so poorly in the past, and sadly in many parts of the world yet today, there has arisen what I would caricature as a "radical feminism", truly an illusion that is profoundly damaging to women. This "radical feminism" is quite different from a true "Christian feminism". The radical form of feminism denies any aspect of complementarity between the sexes. A true and authentic Christian Feminism would take Mary, the mother of Jesus, as its model. Radical Feminism seems to drive the themes of Dan Brown in his fictional book, The DiVinci Code. This book suggests that it is fictional, but sadly goes on to use real names of organizations such as Opus Dei and the Catholic Church. If that were not bad enough, it then misrepresents and at times inaccurately presents the teachings and practices of the Catholic faith and its organizations. The main story line is a supposed conspiratorial cover-up that has been systematically orchestrated for nearly 2000 years by the organized church! Brown's sources are readily available, but have been dismissed as unreliable historical documents.

Many find Brown's book amazing and it raises many interesting questions in their minds. I find it incredible that so many could take it at all seriously. I think one need to look no farther than what the book narrates to be at the center of its most sacred ritual. Namely, the leader of the organization having sexual relations amidst a voyeuristic crowd, while striving for mutual simultaneous orgasm! This is the "divine encounter". Compare this with the likes of Mother Theresa and her outreach to the poorest of poor or John Paul II in is instrumental role in the collapse of Communism in the 20th century. Honestly, which seems to be something that is truly ordered towards the benefit of humanity? Not just an individual, but all of humanity. The Church's fundamental mission is to take Christ to the ends of the earth so that His presence can be recognized in every genetically complete human being, from the earliest stages of embryonic development to the aged and infirmed. It goes back to the story of the emperor and his set of clothes! How can so many people fail to grasp the importance of human dignity and the value of human life?

Another illusion is to believe that by politics and power, there can be justice. There is great injustice in the world. One need only travel to a third or even fourth world country and experience it first hand. Many draw simple conclusions and turn to violence and revolution to bring about justice. In fact, that approach only leads to a change in sides: the oppressed now become the oppressors.

There was a movement in the Church in the mid to late part of last century. It was generally called Liberation Theology. It essentially adopted Marxist ideology and tended to project evil on only the structures of society, instead of recognizing the real source of evil, corrupt individuals in such structures. If one looks at those regions where liberation theology tried to change structures, one finds few schools or hospitals or the conditions improved. I recall a story about some well-intentioned Catholic missionaries. They were traveling to a place where conditions were certainly unjust. It was a religious sister who asked the people what they wanted from the missionaries. The people requested a place to pray; they wanted a church. The religious sister seemed to be dissatisfied with the answer so she asked again, "You must not understand, what do you really want?" They simply returned the same answer emphatically, "We want a place to pray!" The religious became angry and told the people that they really wanted delivered from their oppression and poverty! Sadly the sister missed the point. If our hearts are converted, the world will want our joy and peace, and true justice will be served. Peace will never merely be a cessation of hostility, but will be the result of deep, mutual, and profound respect. We must empower people to defend themselves, but we should never encourage them to become the aggressors. In the Gospel it is clear that Jesus never saw real freedom in terms of some political future.

I will always remember my trip to Nigeria where between 400 and 600 people would celebrate daily mass at 5:30 am. Many had been praying since 4:30 am in the morning. This is the faith that will conquer all oppression and injustice. It may take time, but God will cause the wicked to be vanquished. Hopefully the next generation of leaders will be drawn from those people who are fostering a life of devotion.

The world seems to have adopted a different faith, faith that is rooted in self. There is no transcendence, no real hope for a future after death. Political ends and power for the moment is what motivates many. Much of western society believes that it can fashion a world were truth is subject to the majority opinion. When it comes to social structures there is nothing to be discovered, but there is much to artificially engineer. No perfect feminism or a politics of power or even some super will that can "make reality" will succeed for a stable future. The next chapter looks at the family and human sexuality and how society has failed to grasp its fundamental import.

Chapter V · The Family
and its politically correct
<u>Derivatives</u>

The love that Jesus has for us is revealed in the moral behavior that He sets out in principle. Human sexuality is, I believe, the greatest gift that God has given to the human person this side of heaven. I can remember having a conversation with a friend who came to visit me in my first assignment as a priest. We were talking about family life and he shared the sentiment that I had just mentioned about the gift of human sexuality. He continued by noting that the only way that we could offer anything back to God for the great gift of human sexuality, was by making sure that the gift of sex was open to life. By having this openness to life the person has the real opportunity in sharing with God's creating power. This is made manifest when the gift of another future human being comes into the world. We as humans have something that is unique in that we can make a sacrifice and be fully aware of what that sacrifice means. Marriage is at the heart of God's plan for humanity. In the eyes of God, marriage is not merely something that is good, it is indeed holy and sacred. Jesus summarizes this teaching well in the 19th Chapter of Matthew when He describes God's purpose for man and woman from the beginning. It seems again, in an attempt to trip up Jesus, the religious leaders of the time ask Jesus about divorce. Jesus' response is clear: from the beginning it was intended that the man should leave his father and mother and cling to his wife. The two should become one! I am amazed at some in the religious community who make the outrageous claim that Jesus never made his position clear on homosexuality. Jesus never said that circles are round and blocks are square, but that does not leave the question open for debate. It is obvious, and it is obvious because Jesus wants what is best for all of us. We really are talking about the emperor and his new clothes, or lack thereof. A homosexual orientation is not sinful, any more than a heterosexual orientation is sinful. However, homosexual acts are sinful as are heterosexual acts outside of marriage. There has been a lot in the news about marriage these days and what it is. Marriage is at the heart of being a family for a whole host of reasons.

In his early writings, John Paul II noted *that the future of humanity passes by way of the family.*[31] A spirited debate has raged and is raging over same-sex unions. Let us for a moment remove sexual orientation from the question and reflect on this for a moment. If two individuals were friends and decided to live together in a totally platonic relationship, and yet would want to have the benefits of being family (e.g. hospital visits, insurance benefits, etc) it would seem to me that this could be easily arranged legally through mutual adoption of the other or the appropriate legal documents delineating such things. However this is not what the issue is for some, although they set this up as the pretense. They want to call something a marriage that is not a marriage. A true marriage can only be accomplished by a man and a woman who intend to have children or are open to that possibility, like Abraham and Sara in the Hebrew Scriptures. This is what the purpose of marriage is. It provides a stable unit or safe haven for humans to grow and be nurtured. People are free to call a grape a peach, but calling a grape a peach does not make it so! Hopefully we will be insightful enough to see the reality as it is, and not buckle under to a very small special interest group that ultimately is very confused and misguided, and ultimately promoting behavior that is, in itself, detrimental to psychological and physical well being. The Church is not against those persons who have a homosexual orientation; in fact it recognizes that such an orientation is not sinful. It does maintain that sexual union that is not open to life, and cannot provide a stable environment for children, if they

---

31 *Familiaris Consortio*, n. 86, http://www.vatican.va/holy_father/john_paul_ii/apost_exhortations/documents/hf_jp_ii_exh_19811122_familiaris_consortio_en.html, November 1981.

should be conceived, is immoral, always, without exception. Human sexual union has both a dimension that brings two people intimately close while at the same time is open to life. You see, the church puts humanity first. All humans are equal in God's sight, and it is not for us to determine which human is better than another.

At the heart of human sexual relations is a person's capacity to be so self-possessed that the individual may bring the greatest joy and pleasure to their respective spouse. It must never be merely an act of self-gratification - which some would even go to the extent of calling this rape. This self mastery also sheds light on the Church's prohibition against masturbation. One need not willfully give into temptations to release sexual tension, but through self-mastery, one prepares one self to have the ability to enter into sexual relations on a deeper level than just base instinct. Again in the early writings of John Paul II in the papal audiences on the theology of the Body, he demonstrates how such self-mastery makes this quite clear. It was also misunderstood by the mainstream media that the pope was saying that a husband was not to lust after his wife. This is true, but lust must never be confused with legitimate sexual desire. If a man loses sexual desire for his wife or vise versa it is a tragic thing. Lust is when a person sees the other as merely an object to be consumed or used. In this case the person is not loved and cherished, but merely used.

St. Augustine often gets a bad rap for his views on marriage. Clearly his ideas are not as developed as John Paul II, but John Paul II had the benefit of an additional 1600 years of reflection. Nonetheless Augustine noted that if a person was just having sex with his or her spouse to ease the sexual urge, then the person was committing a venial sin. I cannot imagine any woman liking the idea that her husband was just using her to facilitate a biological release. Sex must always be related to love and life.

Husbands and wives who are pure of heart want their sexual relations to be joy-filled for the other. In turn hopefully the individual will be joy-filled, but the Christian motive lies in serving the other. A woman may want to please her husband and it is conceivable that she might do things that please him, fellatio for example, but this is something that is beneath the dignity of the woman, and any self respecting man would not use a woman in this way. It is a perversion, plain and simple. Society turns this concept, self-possession in order to more completely make a gift on oneself to the other, on its head. It promotes the "use" of another, and this use is epitomized when artificial contraception becomes the norm in marital relations. In fact, it could be argued that sexual relations when using artificial contraception are sinful for the same reason that homosexual relations are sinful. Some forms of homosexual relations, however, are sinful in other dimensions as well, namely the physical damage that is caused by not using the sexual faculties as they were designed by nature to be used. Sodomy for example ruptures blood vessels and physically damages the human body. This adds to the sinful character of homosexual acts. Sin is sin because it hurts the human person. In female acts there is also a singular degree of self-absorption that in the very least is psychologically damaging. There is no hope for fruitfulness in homosexual acts. The definition of sin in the Catechism of the Catholic Church is quite telling:

> *Sin is an offense against reason, truth, and right conscience;*
> *it is failure in genuine love for God and neighbor caused by a*
> *perverse attachment to certain goods. It wounds the nature*
> *of man and injures human solidarity. It has been defined*
> *as "an utterance, a deed, or a desire contrary to the eternal*
> *law.*[32]

Among the crisis in the late 1990's in the Church, many point to the declining numbers in the Catholic Church and often site celibacy as the real culprit. In a study reported in Congregations Magazine in March/April of 2001, the statistics seem to counter this argument. While it is true that priests under the age of 35 have declined in the Catholic Church, they have declined far more rapidly in the Episcopal Church over the same period. In fact this seems strikingly odd in light of what is often presented in the media or what many self-proclaimed progressives would have you believe; they seem to suggest that if only the Church would "get with the times and let priests marry, ordain practicing homosexuals and deny any problem

---

32 **Catechism of the Catholic Church**, n 1849

with divorce and remarriage, the priesthood would be thriving." This point is radically refuted by the one particular denomination that has done just that, yet their clergy by some accounts have fallen from 24% under age 35 in 1975 to less than 4% in 2000.[33] Again people are unwilling or just unaware of the facts. It is sometimes difficult to get accurate statistics, but the ultimate point is that one never benefits from rejecting the truth. The Church strives to foster those things which have humanity's best interest at heart. The Catholic Church is bound by what she believes and has professed to be the truth for some two millennia.

Many people are seemingly so confused over the homosexual issues and this sadly even extends to some members if not many members of the clergy. I was deeply saddened when a fellow priest, who I believe has a great heart, but nonetheless a confused one, seemed to fail to recognize how important the distinction between marriage and civil unions between people of the same sex is. This poor guy wrote an article to the local paper promoting same sex unions. I do not question his intentions for a moment. I believe he has a great heart, but he is very wrong. I offer the following as a reflection that would demonstrate the wisdom and truth that lies behind the Catholic Church's teaching and it was generally my response (that the paper did not publish) with a few additions to this poor misguided soul.

Is Common Sense really a thing of the Past? - On Same Sex Marriage.

We live in a great country where freedom is valued and esteemed like nothing else. Unfortunately, there are intrinsic characteristics of the human person that result in society having to make certain laws that are never intended to curb real freedom. In reality our system strives to protect true freedom. Many people often confuse true freedom as a license to do what ever they want, this sounds good in theory, but in reality it does not really serve humanity or the common good. There are certain things that people realize are just plain wrong. I think it is safe

---

33 Statistics presented from a study by a professor at Concordia Seminary, in Fort Wayne Indiana at a Serra Club meeting.

to say that no one has any problems with laws against rape. If they do, they should be locked up for the safety of others.

We hear a lot about the right to privacy. Privacy ends where the rights of another begin. One has no right to enslave another in the privacy of their home. One should not be able to rape someone, a child or an adult as the result of some right to privacy. There must be no "right to privacy" that enables one person to harm another. There is a huge problem with how one defines the term. At one point in our great society we recognized the right to enslave another human being! Sadly today we have laws that support the destruction of very young developing humans. Why is this? It is simply because they are not recognized as persons, just like the blacks who were denied such recognition in our not so distant past.

We hear a lot of arguments about Same-Sex Marriage and equal protection under the law, but is this really the right question to be asking? I do not think so! Laws exist for society and to ensure that society may truly flourish. While at the same time, society or the State should not become the master over individuals. Human dignity demands a certain autonomy. As noted, we live in a free country. If someone wants to engage in some behavior that is less than healthy, they should be free to do so, so long as it does not directly impact the health of those around them, (e.g. smoking or eating junk food). Do we really want to live in a society, or some "Brave New World", where one could never enjoy a victory cigar or a piece of cheesecake that is loaded with fat and cholesterol? It is a free country, after all. By the same token, should there be laws suggesting that everyone is obliged to pay for the added health risks that smokers choose to impose upon themselves by their choices? I think not! Should there be a law saying insurers cannot ask, "Do you smoke?" This behavior is known to increase health risks, and, therefore, it is only right that smokers pay higher life and health insurance rates than do non-smokers. This is just simple fairness. It makes sense; there is a certain logic to it all, is there not? But as I said, I am not sure that common sense is so common today.

Leaving religious arguments totally out of the analysis (after all there are some who have confined even people who smoke to the deep regions of hell), it does not take a rocket scientist to figure out that there are intrinsic risks in homosexual relationships both to society and the individual. This is simply the facts; one can even find such statistics from organizations that are very sympathetic to the homosexual cause. Ask any proctologist for his honest opinion about male homosexual relations and the damage that it can cause. The detrimental effects can be substantiated by the clinical data. We live in a society that protects humans and affords them rights to do things that even harm themselves. We do not seem to be very consistent even in this. I can be arrested for not wearing a seat belt, but I guess the police need something to generate revenues. Generally speaking, a person is free to eat junk food, smoke a cigar or even engage in mutually destructive behavior between consenting adults. This, however, should never be seen as something that needs to be recognized or legitimized. For example: making laws that say, "Smoking is as healthy and normal as not smoking!" "Anyone who can not see this is a smokaphobe and racist!" Isn't that frankly silly? Oops, I keep forgetting, common sense is not so common!

Sound scientific data constrained by the real pursuit of truth, and not merely a political agenda, will certainly confirm the following conclusion. The fundamental building block for a stable, healthy, and vibrant society is a family that is stable and is a forum for sound psychological development for its members. No one can rationally argue against the fact that a family, a man and a woman, both with unique physical and psychological attributes, provide the ideal environment for nurturing and fostering the healthy psychological development of children. This arrangement has been recognized since antiquity as a legal arrangement called Marriage. Society benefits from such an arrangement and should pass, and has passed, laws recognizing the value of such an arrangement. Historically, these are the essential aspects in marriage; not love, or self-contentment, or self-fulfillment, but this legal arrangement which benefits society with stability and the means for society to continue by the repopulation of its members.

We live in a country that enables people to make choices despite their own ability to make good choices for their optimal health. A good society should never make laws to encourage irresponsible or detrimental behavior. In fact, it should try and curb or, at the very least, discourage destructive behavior when possible. The popular taxes on alcohol and tobacco reflect this. These are often pejoratively called a "sin tax." Smokers are people, but they have made choices that place them in a different category and share different health risks than do non-smokers, and, in fact, have demonstrated their willingness to pay for their vice. There are distinctions that are made. There must also be distinctions made for those persons who choose to enter into same-sex unions. They are a distinct category from "married couples". Again, this is just a conclusion one must make out of fairness to all involved. Society is to make laws that will help preserve or stabilize it. The laws should be those that benefit the social structure. It would be grossly irresponsible for society to make laws that somehow suggest smoking is not hazardous to your health. Likewise, it would be equally irresponsible for society to put forth the pretense that same sex unions are the same as marriage. It is bad law for society and the individuals who may not be responsible enough, or knowledgeable enough, or insightful enough, to suggest there is no difference between a domestic partnership, as it is often called, and marriage. Persons should not be encouraged to follow such a lifestyle by bad law.

The issue is not conservative, or liberal, religious or pagan, but just common sense, but as is seemingly more and more apparent, common sense is not so common. This is sad, but obviously very true. I had served in a pastoral situation where many people struggled with their sexual orientation. It was truly and clearly a cross for them. Life is not always fair, but God is always just. The real beauty of the Church's teaching is that it will never condemn individuals for their inclinations, but rather challenge them to be selfless and practice heroic virtue. True compassion is never manifest by encouraging sin or self-destructive behavior. From the etymology of the word, the person who is truly compassionate is the person who has the capacity to "suffer with" someone. You walk with the person; you do not lie to him or her and say that there is nothing harmful, when in fact there is something that is detrimental to the human person. All sin is analogous to a cancer that is tearing into the fabric of our society. In many, like cancer, sin often goes unnoticed and undetected, but it continues to weaken and harm the healthy body. We must be open enough to recognize that which is truly good for us and our neighbor.

One of the things that is most frustrating for me, and I suspect for parents, is to see their children make mistakes that are setting them up for great hardship. Many politically correct positions are ultimately very self destructive. There may be satisfaction for the moment, but the long term implications are enormous. It really does come down to charity for others. How much do we really care? We have been inundated with the idea, "look out for number one", but if we fail to look out for others, there will be no future "number ones" to look out for! We will have destroyed any sense of human dignity that we truly have as an innate instinct. Children learn to hate others. Hatred is a learned behavior, love is innate.

If we hope to thrive as a society, we must be willing to not live in the world of illusion and deception. We must strive to recapture that which will make our society more stable and viable. It really is as simple as seeing things as they are. Recognizing that people really are the most precious natural resource our world has to offer. The key truly lies in the family as the fundamental building block for all social order.

To quote John Paul II in the document *Familiaris Consortio*[34], "The future of humanity passes by way of the family". In the next chapter is my attempt to relate the key aspects of the excellent reflection John Paul offered on the family.

---

34 John Paul II, *Familiaris Consortio*, Apostolic Exhortation, n. 86, 1981.

CHAPTER VI · JOHN PAUL II
ON THE FAMILY

In this chapter I would like to take a more thorough look at John Paul II's reflection on the family. I think it is very helpful to walk through the document and attempt to relate the richness and insight of his thoughts.

The introduction of the document *Familiaris Consortio* assesses the current situation. It recognizes the rapid changes in the world, along with the great confusion and controversy regarding the ultimate purpose of conjugal family life.

The document is addressed to three categories of people:

a) Those that are already aware of the value of married life and seek to live it faithfully.

b) Those who are anxious and uncertain and seeking the truth.

c) Those that are unjustly impeded from freely living their family lives.

The document wishes to support the first group, enlighten the second, and assist the third in dealing with their unjust situations.

The family is an educating community, educating the human person on how to live in community which is rich in justice and in love. The family must be preserved from forms that the world is trying to impose on the family structure.

I. Bright Spots and Shadows for the Family Today

Family life is not something up in the clouds; it touches every person in his or her daily experience. The Church wants to understand the concrete situations in which people find themselves; also, the Church wants to help deepen one's understanding of what it means to be truly human. Jesus Christ is fully human and fully divine. In theological language, Jesus is a divine person, Jesus being the only one who has both a human nature and a divine nature. To be truly and fully human is to live the way Jesus lived. Jesus' humanity is to be used as the model for the way we live out our own humanity. Some people who see humanity in a less positive light hold out solutions that seem appealing but actually are not becoming or adequate in revealing the true dignity of the human person; therefore, the supposed solutions give a skewed reflection of the Divine in relation to the human.

The Church recognizes that the mass media can subtly endanger freedom and make it more difficult to make an objective judgment. In other words, opinions based not on Christ and His human nature and all its implications are put forth as solutions, but are totally inadequate.

When the Church refers to freedom, freedom must not be confused with license to do anything one desires or wants. Real freedom is our capacity to become truly what God intended us to be loving, gentle, and merciful human beings. A bunny rabbit is not free to become a cat; likewise we are limited in a certain sense to be nothing less than truly human. The tyrants of history are marked by their inhumanity, not their humanity! This idea of freedom presumes a faith: a faith in God and a faith in the instrument that God has left us, namely the Church. It is through the Church we can reliably interpret His revelation and be guided by His revelation.

God has given many different gifts to His people. These charisms are made manifest in many different ways. Different people with various gifts work together to more fully reveal the activity of God's Word, the Mystical Body of Christ, in the world.

The document is developing the idea of the *sensus fidelis*, the supernatural sense of the faithful. This supernatural sense is not limited to just the pastors; it includes others who share in the membership of God's community. The sense of the faithful does not solely consist in the consensus of the people; that is to say that it is not simply a majority rules situation. As the document states:

> *She listens to conscience, not to power.... Pastors for their part must: promote the sense of the faith in all the faithful, examine and authoritatively judge the genuineness of its expression, and educate the faithful in an ever more mature evangelical discernment.*[35]

The family situation can reflect one of two things, the first being a sign of salvation of Christ operating in the world (a truly effective sacrament), or, to the contrary, a sign of the refusal that the human person gives to the love of God.

An Effective Sacrament

- A more lively awareness of personal freedom (freedom to be truly human as Christ was) and greater attention to interpersonal relationships in marriage
- Promotion of the dignity of women
- Responsible procreation
- Education of children
- Recognition to foster interfamily relationships
- Truly a give-and-take attitude when it comes to both material and spiritual goods
- A true deepening awareness of the family's obligation to proclaim the gospel of Christ by the way it lives
- The family's recognition of contributing to a just society

---

35 *Familiaris Consortio*, n. 5

Signs of Weakening of Some Fundamental Family Values

- A mistaken theoretical concept of the independence between the spouses in relation to one another
- Serious misconceptions regarding the relationship of authority between parents and children
- The concrete difficulty families experience in attempting to transmit family values
- The growing numbers of divorces
- The scourge of abortion
- The more frequent recourse to sterilization
- The appearance of a truly contraceptive mentality

The document states that what lies at the root of these problems is a mistaken idea of freedom, "conceived not as a capacity for realizing the truth of God's plan for marriage and the family, but as an autonomous power of self-affirmation, often against others, for one's own selfish well being."

In fact, the document observes that the developed countries, those who experience great prosperity and typically have a consumer mentality, paradoxically experience a certain anguish and uncertainty about the future. Ironically those who are seemingly most economically secure are often deprived of a generosity and the courage needed for raising up new human life. Even though many in this economic situation are able to support new life, they shy away from the challenge to be open to life. Thus it happens that children are not perceived as a blessing but rather as a danger from which one is to be defended.

Some people today mistakenly think that historically we are assured of progress, a slow progression to what is better. In reality, it is an event of freedom and even a struggle between conflicting interests. The document refers to Augustine as he relates the conflict between two loves, "the love of God to the point of disregarding self and the love of self to the point of disregarding God." Ultimately the family needs to be engaged in building an authentic humanism, a humanism that is rooted in the human nature of Christ. This is not the human nature to which the world crassly adheres; a humanism not rooted in Christ, but rooted in the deformed, sin-filled, fallen nature of unredeemed man.

More Troubling Signs (n. 7)

- The spread of divorce and recourse to a new union, even on the part of the faithful
- An acceptance of purely civil marriage in contradiction to the vocation of the baptized to "be married in the Lord"
- The celebration of the marriage sacrament without a living faith but for other motives
- The rejection of the moral norms that guide and promote the human and Christian in the exercise of sexuality in marriage

What must the Church do?

The document states:The whole Church is obliged to a deep reflection and commitment so that the new culture now emerging may be evangelized in depth, true values acknowledged, the rights of men and women defended, and justice promoted in the very structures of society.[36]

Needs

- Science needs to serve the human person
- Our era needs such wisdom more than bygone ages if the discoveries made by man are to be further humanized
- Recover the primacy of moral values by educating the moral conscience
- Modern culture must be led to a more profoundly restored covenant with Divine Wisdom
- Continuous, permanent conversion, to lead God's faithful ever closer

---

36 *ibid*, n. 8.

- "Inculturation" of Christian values needs to become ever more wide spread, this is taking the positive steps necessary to form the culture by Christian values. Inculturation is the means by which the full restoration between man and the Wisdom of God will take place

- To be informed by third world cultures that lack technology, but not wisdom, a wisdom which is the fruit of living truly a human way of life

II. The Plan of God for Marriage and the Family

The ideal of family life is intimately bound up in the mystery of God and how God has revealed Himself in human history. A family is a community of persons who share and live in a harmonious communion. God in God's very essence is community. In other words, God is Trinity, Father, Son, and Holy Spirit. God's very essence is *love*. Before there can be real love, there must be something other than oneself to love, whether it be a thing or a person. Love is a mystery but is discernable when there is something else that draws the attention of our own wants and, even perhaps, needs.

God is a lover because of the three persons in the Trinity. Since we are all made in the image and likeness of God, the Christian vocation can be only to love, to be like God, and in fact to be caught up in the very mystery of God Himself. Christian revelation tells us two distinct ways to realize this vocation, either by marriage or the celibate state.

In marriage the spouses give themselves to each other in ways that are *proper and exclusive* to themselves in the married life. It by no means is something purely biological; it touches the human person to the very core and essence of his or her being.

It is realized in a truly human way only if it is an integral part of the love by which a man and a woman commit themselves totally to one another until death. The total physical self-giving would be a lie if it were not the sign and fruit of a total personal self-giving, in which the whole person, including the temporal dimension, is present: if the person were to withhold something or reserve the possibility of deciding otherwise in the future, by this very fact he or she would not be giving totally.[37]

From this concept is a major component in the church's teaching on contraception. Artificial contraception is a limitation of the free and total gift that the spouses have promised of themselves to each other. The document's definition of Marriage:

> *The institution of marriage is not an undue interference by society or authority, not the extrinsic imposition of a form. Rather it is an interior requirement of the covenant of conjugal love which is publicly affirmed as unique and exclusive; in order to live complete fidelity to the plan of God, the Creator. A person's freedom, far from being restricted by this fidelity, is secured against every form of subjectivism or relativism and is made a sharer in creative Wisdom.*[38]

As mentioned before, the plan of marriage is intimately bound to the way God has revealed Himself in human history. Historically God has established **covenants**. Covenants are not merely contracts. To the contrary, by their very essence they do not promise goods for services rendered; they, the covenants, imply relationships, love relationships. God did not say, "Do this, this, and this, or you will go to Hell, or Sheol, or Gehenna." No, God said, "You do this, this, and this, and you will be My people, and I will be your God". The God of the Christian's and Jews is a God of relationship, a God who desires to be united with His creatures in a covenantal bond. It is for this reason that the image of marriage in the scriptures is so often used to relate to the people God's own relationship with them. And more negatively, the infidelity of Israel is reckoned with the behavior of a prostitute or an unfaithful spouse. From the beginning, the true purpose of marriage was revealed: that two should become one, and live in true and harmonious unity.

---

37 *ibid, n. 11*

38 *ibid*, n. 11.

Because marriage is such a profound example of faithful love and ordained by God as such, marriage is revered as a sacrament. Tertullian, an early Christian, gives his own reflection on Christian marriage:

> *How can I ever express the happiness of the marriage that is joined together by the Church, strengthened by an offering, sealed by a blessing, announced by angels and ratified by the Father?... How wonderful the bond between two believers, with a single hope, a single desire, a single observance, a single service! They are both brethren and both fellow-servants; there is no separation between them in spirit or flesh; in fact they are truly two in one flesh, and where the flesh is one, one is the spirit.*[39]

The Church understands marriage as a saving event, a real symbol of the event of salvation. Like every sacrament it is a memorial, actuation, and prophecy.[40]

- As a memorial, the sacrament gives them the grace and duty of commemorating the great works of God and of bearing witness to them before their children.

- As actuation, it gives them the grace and duty of putting into practice in the present, towards each other and their children, the demands of a love which forgives and redeems.

- As prophecy, it gives them the grace and duty of living and bearing witness to the hope of the future encounter with Christ.

---

39 *ibid*, n. 13

40 *ibid*, n. 13.

According to the plan of God, marriage is the foundation of the wider community of the family, since the very institution of marriage and conjugal love are ordained to the procreation and education of children, in whom they (marriage and conjugal love) find their crowning.[41]

Parents' love for their children is a reflection and a visible sign of God's own love. The church recognizes that this is not the only value of conjugal life. For those who are not blessed with children, other avenues are opened that may not have been.

Physical sterility in fact can be for spouses the occasion for other important services to the life of the human person, for example, adoption, various forms of educational work, and assistance to other families and to poor or handicapped children.

The human family is ultimately the way in which people are introduced in the great family of the Church.

The document spends little time on virginity or celibacy, but that is because virginity and celibacy take their great power from the awesome character of the family:

When marriage is not esteemed, neither can consecrated virginity or celibacy exist; when human sexuality is not regarded as a great value given by the Creator, the renunciation of it for the sake of the Kingdom of Heaven loses its meaning...... By virtue of this witness, virginity or celibacy keeps alive in the Church a consciousness of the mystery of marriage and defends it from any reduction and impoverishment.

---

41 *ibid*, n. 14.

> *Virginity or celibacy, by liberating the human heart in a unique way, "so as to make it burn with greater love for God and all humanity,"[42] bears witness that the Kingdom of God and His justice is that pearl of great price which is preferred to every other value no matter how great, and hence must be sought as the only definitive value. It is for this reason that the Church, throughout her history, has always defended the superiority of this charism to that of marriage, by reason of the wholly singular link which it has with the Kingdom of God.....*

> *Christian couples therefore have the right to expect from celibate persons a good example and a witness of fidelity to their vocation until death.[43]*

The document also notes that this reflection may be able to help those who may not have preferred to live a celibate lifestyle, but may nonetheless see the great power in it lived faithfully and embraced in the spirit of service to all of humanity.

One must recognize that the superiority of the gift of celibacy is by no means a reflection on the human person himself or herself. The quality of the human person lies in sharing the nature of Christ, not in any gifts that are freely given by God. We will not be judged by the gifts themselves that we have received but rather by the quality in which we use those gifts from God.

III. The Role of the Christian Family

The family not only finds out what it is because of God's plan, but it also finds its mission or task that it is called to fulfill in the plan of salvation. The family is an intimate community of life and love. Those who see a Christian family, see the very workings of God Himself. The document states:

---

42 Second Vatican Ecumenical Council, Decree on Renewal of Religious Life *Perfectae Caritatis*, 12.

43 *Familiaris Consortio*, n. 16

Hence the family has the mission to guard, reveal and communicate love, and this is a living reflection of and a real sharing in God's love for humanity and the love of Christ the Lord for the Church his Bride.[44]

The general tasks of the family include:

1 - Forming a community of persons
2 - Serving life
3 - Participating in the development of society
4 - Sharing in the life and mission of the Church

Forming a Community of Persons

The church boldly asserts what a family is: "The family, which is founded and given life by love, is a community of persons: of husband and wife, of parents and children, of relatives"; and the family's task: "Its first task is to live with fidelity the reality of communion in a constant effort to develop an authentic community of persons."

The driving force or the thing that is ultimately sought after is *love*. Without love a family is not a community of persons and, in the same way, *without love the family cannot live, grow, and perfect itself as a community of persons*. Love is necessary for the human person. If love is not revealed to the human person, life has no meaning and is senseless. Family life is about being more intensely a community, a *communion*.

This communion first established between husband and wife, grows, deepens, and is reflected more profoundly by the total self gift of one to the other. This is a total gift, not just of physical attributes, but of spirit, soul, and body. The church in her tradition has always recognized the goodness of creation. If God made it, it has to be good. God cannot be the source of any evil in the world. This gift of communion is fostered and made possible by the gift of God's Spirit.

---

44 *ibid.* n. 17.

> *The gift of the Spirit is a commandment of life for Christian spouses and at the same time a stimulating impulse so that every day they may progress towards an ever richer union with each other on all levels - of the body, of the character, of the heart, of the intelligence and will, of the soul"[45] - revealing in this way to the Church and to the world the new communion of love, given by the grace of Christ.[46]*

This radical idea of communion in a new way rules out polygamy, because polygamy is contrary to the equal dignity that men and women in marriage offer the total gift of themselves to each other in a unique and exclusive way.

This radical communion is not only characterized by its unity, but also its indissolubility. God remains faithful and since marriage is an outward sign of this fidelity it cannot be legitimately compromised.

The church respects those who may have been abandoned by their partner and who have not entered into a new union. Great encouragement needs to be offered to these people in their difficult situation.

The communion of the family is fostered by natural means, flesh and blood, but these are brought to human perfection by richer and deeper bonds of the spirit. The family becomes the "school of deeper humanity."[47] This "deeper school" may be realized in the Christian family if parents *exercise their unrenounceable authority as a true and proper "ministry," that is, as a service to the human and Christian well-being of their children, and in particular as a service aimed at helping them acquire a truly responsible freedom, and if parents maintain a living awareness of the "gift" they continually receive from their children.*[48]

The church realistically points out that this idealistic communion can only be perfected through a real spirit of sacrifice. A true vocation

---

45 John Paul II, Address to Married People at Kinshasa (May 3, 1980)

46 *Familiaris Consortio,* n. 19.

47 *Gaudium et Spes*, n. 52.

48 *Familiaris Consortio*, n. 21.

must be fostered for all the members of the family. A true Christian vocation achieves its fullness by a sincere self-giving.

The document emphasizes that this self-giving is shared equally by both men and women.

> *In creating the human race "male and female", God gives man and woman an equal personal dignity, endowing them with the inalienable rights and responsibilities proper to the human person. God then manifests the dignity of women in the highest form possible, by assuming human flesh from the Virgin Mary, whom the Church honors as the Mother of God, calling her the new Eve and presenting her as the model of redeemed woman.*[49]

The document recognizes that women and men share equally in their dignity, and thus women are fully justified in their pursuit of public functions. The church also asserts that true advancement of women requires clear recognition of the value of their maternal and family role, by comparison to all other public roles and other professions. These other legitimate tasks must be harmoniously combined if society is to evolve in a truly human way.[50]

Women have every right to work in public positions but should not be compelled to do so. Society must be structured in such a way that women, in effect, are not penalized by making the choice to spend all their time with their own family.

The heart of the message concerning the dignity of women lies in seeing them not as a human person but rather an object of trade to be used for selfish interest and mere pleasure. Too often this mentality concerning the human person, both men and women, results in:

- Slavery
- Oppression of the weak
- Pornography
- Prostitution - especially in an organized form

---

49 *ibid*, n. 22.

50 *ibid*, n. 23.

- Forms of discrimination that exist in the fields of education, employment, wages, etc.

The council fathers condemn such discrimination in all its heinous forms. Positively they look to Ambrose for an authentic view of conjugal life and an attitude towards one's wife:

> *You are not her master, but her husband; she was not given to you to be your slave, but your wife...Reciprocate her attentiveness to you and be grateful to her for her love.[51]*

A clear priority is given to a normative structure, (husband - wife) with the following reasoning from the same paragraph as Ambrose's comment:

> *.. the absence of a father causes psychological and moral imbalance and notable difficulties in family relationships, as does, in contrary circumstances, the oppressive presence of a father, especially where there still prevails the phenomenon of "machismo", or a wrong superiority of male prerogatives which humiliates women and inhibits the development of healthy family relationships.*

The Family's role in Serving Life

Transmission of Life

The document uses the word fecundity, this means fruitfulness; in other words, marriage is to be productive.

> *Fecundity is the fruit and the sign of conjugal love, the living testimony of the full reciprocal self-giving of the spouses: "While not making the other purposes of matrimony of less account, the true practice of conjugal love, and the whole meaning of the family life which results from it, have this*

---

51 *ibid*, n. 25

> *aim: that the couple be ready with stout hearts to cooperate*
> *with the love of the Creator and the Savior, who through*
> *them will enlarge and enrich his own family day by day.*"[52]

The Church is putting forth a very high ideal that is rooted in the fact that this world is passing away. Therefore we must understand that Christians are not to serve the world, but rather that the presence of Christians in the world is to transform it into a community that preserves and protects the great dignity of the human person, a dignity that is rooted in the nature of Jesus Christ. It is mind blowing to realize that Jesus' divine nature remains fully intact as He lived and lives both then and now!

The document reaffirms the earlier encyclical, *Humanae Vitae*, in its respect and recognition and reaffirmation of the teaching that "love between husband and wife must be fully human, exclusive, and open to new life."[53] The Church is critical of those attitudes that see scientific advancement as a good only designed to master nature with little regard for the infinite dignity that each human person possesses. In the name of science and the concern for the world, techniques and approaches are utilized that disregard the child to be born or the intrinsic nature, and hence the value of the human person. In underdeveloped nations contraceptive techniques, including abortion, are imposed on people because population control is mistakenly seen as an ***ultimate*** good. Some countries are beginning to realize the threat to their own future by such policies. These contraceptive efforts lead to an anti-life mentality, the letter states:

> *Thus an anti-life mentality is born, as can be seen in many*
> *current issues: one thinks, for example, of a certain panic*
> *deriving from the studies of ecologist and futurologists on*
> *population growth which sometimes exaggerate the danger of*
> *demographic increase to the danger of life........*

---

52 Vatican II Document on the Church in the Modern World, *Gaudium et Spes*, n. 50.

53 *Humanae Vitae*, n. 11.

> *Thus the Church condemns as a grave offense against human dignity and justice all those activities of governments or other public authorities which attempt to limit in any way the freedom of couples in deciding about children. Consequently any violence applied by such authorities in favor of contraception or, still worse, of sterilization and procured abortion, must be altogether condemned and forcefully rejected.*

The document condemns also any economic pressure that is applied in favor of contraceptive practices. The world community is badly misled in its attempts to help the world by embracing such an anti-life mentality.

The Church reaffirms its teaching on the prohibition of artificial contraceptive techniques and invites theologians to help persuade the world community of the soundness of these policies which respect life. The Church always appreciates the singular importance of each and every human person. The human person is the only creature that has the capacity to care for the goods of the earth, and no one has the right to deprive another human person of something only God can give, LIFE.

There exists such a distorted view of the human person. The true meaning of sexuality is gravely distorted and misinterpreted by much of the culture. Sexuality is not something which is defined solely by the person or his or her intentions. The Church presents "sexuality as a value and task of the whole person, created male and female in the image of God."

The document spends some space in reflection on the moral aspect of harmonizing conjugal love with the transmission of life.

> *...the moral aspect of any procedure does not depend solely on sincere intentions or on an evaluation of motives. It must be determined by objective standards. These, based on the nature of the human person and his or her acts, preserve the full sense of mutual self-giving and human procreation in the context of true love. Such a goal cannot be achieved unless the virtue of conjugal chastity is sincerely practiced."[54]*

---

54 *Gaudium et Spes*, n. 51.

Responsible parenthood includes two aspects in Catholic teaching, the unitive aspect and the procreative aspect. In other words the husband and wife come together (unitive) to form the heart of the community of persons. This unity must contribute to harmony and have an openness to fruitfulness (procreative). When married couples separate these aspects "that God the Creator has inscribed in the being of man and woman" by resorting to contraception ", they act as "arbiters" of the divine plan and "manipulate" and degrade human sexuality. One must recognize the fundamental difference in the human person's intervention in the act of sexual relations and the human person's intervention in other medical matters. Science's noble task is to help something function appropriately; surgery is to make something better or save one's mortal life. Artificial contraception, when used, frustrates nature; it attempts to destroy or degrade the functioning of the human body. It is something quite unique in the practice of modern medicine.

The document, *Humanae Vitae*, recognizes that in certain cases it is allowable to resort to natural methods (NFP) to regulate birth. This is definitively different than artificial methods of contraception:

> *When instead, by means of recourse to periods of infertility, the couple respect the inseparable connection between the unitive and the procreative meanings of human sexuality, they are acting as "ministers" of God's plan and they "benefit from" their sexuality according to the original dynamism of "total" self-giving, without manipulation or altercation.*

Natural methods in regulating birth involve accepting the cycle of the person, that is the woman, and thereby accepting dialogue, reciprocal respect, shared responsibility, and self-control. If one considers these attributes, one sees that these are truly needed for healthy and mature relationships.

The Church believes this teaching to be emphatically true, and therefore takes her responsibility as both teacher and mother quite seriously. It is out of love for her children that the Church tirelessly attests to these truths.

The Church knows the situation of her children well and understands the great challenges that this teaching presents but, nonetheless, believes that her insight is far from harming conjugal life but rather confers a higher meaning to married love. The Church recognizes that this demands virtue, something to which we are all called to strive.

John Paul II made a distinction between the *law of gradualness* and what some would want to confuse as the *gradualness of law*. The Church believes that truth is truth and not dependent upon the person's knowledge of that truth. The law of gradualness recognizes that our insight into the truth is often a gradual process, and therefore we may not be able to understand the truth fully and therefore not act in full accord with that truth. In that case one's own inability to grasp the fullness of the truth may lead him or her to act wrongly, with less moral guilt. The *gradualness of law* is an incorrect understanding that would suggest that one's own limited or "gradual" knowledge of the truth somehow defines or makes legitimate something that is objectively wrong. This may seem like a minor point, but it makes a tremendous amount of difference. The *law of gradualness* encourages one to strive for deeper insight so that he or she may live more in accord with the truth, while the *gradualness of law* has no such internal motivation. One would be actually content not to deepen his or her knowledge, because deeper knowledge would then introduce him or her to more serious obligations. This section is summed up with a closing quote by Paul VI:

> *To them the Lord trusts the task of making visible to people the holiness and sweetness of the law which unites the mutual love of husband and wife with their cooperation with the love of God the author of human life.*

Education

Parents have a fundamental obligation to educate their children. In fact the Church sees the parents as being the ones primarily responsible for the education of their children. Parents must help their children to understand Christian values and help them to have a correct understanding of reality. Society's views are often times less than adequate, especially when many fail to grasp the distinction to be truly free as opposed to have the licence to do anything a person would like to do. The document states:

> *Children must grow up with a correct attitude of freedom with regard to material goods, by adopting a simple and austere lifestyle and being fully convinced that "man is more precious for what he is than for what he has".*[55] ...... *The family is the first and fundamental school of social living: as a community of love, it finds in self-giving the law that guides it and makes it grow.*

Parents have the obligation to help their children understand sexuality also in terms of the whole person:

> *...the educational service of parents must aim firmly at training in the area of sex that is truly and fully personal: for sexuality is an enrichment of the whole person - body, emotions and soul - and it manifests its inmost meaning in leading the person to the gift of self in love.*

The document speaks of the law of subsidiarity in dealing with sex education. What this means is that since parents are the primary educators of their children, those institutions, which share in the education of the children, must be secondary and submissive to the will of the parents. In other words, the schools have no right to teach children values that run contrary to the teachings of the Church, and therefore the parents have an obligation to see that their children clearly understand true Christian values not only in other fields but in the areas that concern sexuality as well.

Children must come to appreciate the meaning of *chastity* and its value: how virginity and celibacy witness to the kingdom of God and how these alternative lifestyles show forth the power of the Gospel of Jesus Christ in different ways.

The mission of the parents to educate their children is truly a "ministry". St. Thomas Aquinas compares the task of the parents to educate with the same task that the priest has. [n. 38] The second

---

55 *Gaudium et Spes*, n. 35.

Vatican council describes the content of Christian education as follows:

> *Such an education does not merely strive to foster maturity...*
> *in the human person. Rather, its principal aims are these:*
> *that as baptized persons are gradually introduced into a*
> *knowledge of the mystery of salvation, they may daily grow*
> *more conscious of the gift of faith which they have received;*
> *that they may learn to adore God the Father in spirit and in*
> *truth (cf. Jn 4:23), especially through liturgical worship; that*
> *they may be trained to conduct their personal life in true*
> *righteousness and holiness, according to their new nature*
> *(Eph 4:22-24), and thus grow to maturity, to the stature of*
> *the fullness of Christ(cf. Eph 4:13), and devote themselves*
> *to the up building of the Mystical Body. Moreover, aware of*
> *their calling, they should grow accustomed to giving witness*
> *to the hope that is in them (cf. 1 Pt 3:15), and to promoting*
> *the Christian transformation of the world.*[56]

Familiaris Consortio also noted that the Synod fathers hoped that a *Catechism for Families* be provided to help the family in their task. [n. 39] This document preceded the publication of the Catechism of the Catholic Church, a reference document that is tremendously valuable in determining what the Church really teaches.

The family is the primary but not the exclusive educating community. For that reason more cooperation and collaboration need to be accomplished between the family and the society at large. This is done by the parents fulfilling their serious obligation to involve themselves with the schools and the schools activities. Parents need to help children see the truth and falsehood that is presented to them from other institutions of learning. [n. 40]

In summary then, the parents have an incredible responsibility to transmit life in all dimensions. It goes much further than fulfilling the basic needs of physical survival. Responsible parenthood entails fulfilling the needs that provide access to eternal life.

---

56 Apostolic Exhortation, *Evangelii Nuntiandi*, n. 71.

Participating in the Development of Society

The family is "the first and vital cell of society."[57] The family is the school where people learn to be human or inhuman as the case may be. The family must be a place to strive for radical communion, a place where relationships are fostered and nourished. It is the family that holds the key in ultimately "humanizing" our world.

> *Consequently, faced with a society that is running the risk of becoming more and more depersonalized and standardized and therefore inhuman and dehumanizing, with the negative results of many forms of escapism - such as alcoholism, drugs and even terrorism - the family possesses and continues still to release formidable energies capable of taking the human person out of his or her anonymity, keeping him or her conscious of his or her personal dignity, enriching him or her, in his or her uniqueness and unrepeatability, within the fabric of society.[58]*

Even though the family's primary and irreplaceable form of expression is procreation and education, it cannot stop there. The social role of the family includes a dedication to "manifold social service activities, especially in favor of the poor, or at any rate for the benefit of all people and situations that cannot be reached by the public authorities' welfare organizations."[59]

The family must grow in its own awareness of how important it is and be prepared to defend its own rights and become evermore active in the transformation of society. *Familiaris Consortio* notes the Second Vatican Council's call to go beyond an **indivualistic ethic.**[60]

---

57 Second Vatican Ecumenical Council, Decree on the Apostolate of the Laity, *Apostolicam Actuositatem*, n. 11.

58 *Familiaris Consortio*, n. 43.

59 *ibid*, n. 44.

60 *Gaudium et Spes*, n. 30, <u>The Church in the Modern World</u>.

Society for its part must always be in service of the family. This Apostolic Exhortation further reflects on the idea of "subsidiarity." This relates to having priorities in line. The society must never perceive itself to be more important than the human person or the family. The government must exist as a means to preserve the common good of all. Clearly communistic regimes and socialist regimes often subjugate the family as merely a structure to serve the state. This should never be the case. Society therefore has an obligation to serve the family by seeing that its most basic needs are met and not perceive the family as something to serve the state. In fact, a **Charter of Family Rights**, a list of 14 items, found in paragraph n. 46, was put forth among the synod pastors.

The document's portrayal of the family is made more discernable by also grasping the church's understanding of the sacrament of marriage, an outward manifestation of two people's sacrificial love for one another that is an image of God's own love for God's people. Like God, who throughout history has concretely involved Himself with His people, so too married couples have serious obligations to involve themselves in the world so that God and God's ways can be "incarnated". The Incarnation is God becoming man in the person of Jesus Christ. Christ invites us to be one with Him [Jn 20:17] in His Mystical Body, the Body of Christ, the Church. Insofar as the family is one with Christ, Christ is truly present in that community of persons.

Sharing in the Life and Mission of the Church

The family must take on its mission by being that community of life and love. The family's ultimate goal is to be a true Christian community, a foundational church. There must always be a dynamic struggle for unity and peace, of oneness of mind and heart, of fidelity and fruitfulness. The Christian family is called to be: 1) a believing and evangelizing community, 2) a community in dialogue with God, and 3) a community at the service of the human person.[61]

---

61 *Familiaris Consortio, ibid*, n. 50.

Believing and Evangelizing Community

This entails an "obedience of faith," a recognition that a family must allow itself to be formed by the Gospel of Jesus Christ, the Gospel that permeates the family and enables it to radiate the love of God and the love of the human person. In places where governments do not allow the study of the Gospel or where the din or noise of a secular materialistic, selfish society drown out the Gospel values, the family is a secure haven to learn and develop a more profound understanding of what it means to love.

Parents must understand that by forming their children to be people who love, they are really and truly ministering to the Church. The missionary activity of the family need not be limited to members of their own family but are encouraged to witness as a true community of persons to those outside the familial bounds.

A Community in Dialogue with God

The family shares in the priestly role of Christ as they pray and offer their lives in service of the other family members. By this activity they are "called to be sanctified and to sanctify the ecclesial community and the world."

Marriage in this sacramental sense in itself is an act of worship. Sacramental married love is an image of God's selfless love for His people. Like the Eucharist, the ultimate Sacrament of unity, marriage participates in the unity of the radical communion that the spouses share.

God, throughout the ages, has shown His mercy to His people again and again. In a broken world, where sin is a reality, families have a need to be an image of God's forgiveness and reconciliation and receive God's mercy when they have fallen into sin.

Family prayer is so important. If any relationship is to last, communication is the core necessity. Prayer is communication with God. Prayer at the family level takes on a special significance. The very essence of family life is to be an image of the community of persons of the Holy Trinity. The family's purpose is to *communicate* this reality to the world. This will be more effectively communicated as the family grows in its own awareness of its great importance. This is accomplished through prayer, both private prayer and participation in Liturgical, formal Ecclesial (church) prayer. For Catholics, the prayer of the family rosary is strongly recommended. Prayer, meditation, whatever one calls it, is an important part of being human.

> *Indeed, prayer is an important part of our very humanity: it is "the first expression of Man's inner truth, the first condition for authentic freedom of spirit."*[62]

Service to God and to the Human Person

The law of Christian life is to be found not in a written code, but in the personal action of the Holy Spirit who inspires and guides the Christian. It is the "Law of the Spirit of life in Christ Jesus". [Rom 8:2] "God's love has been poured into our hearts through the Holy Spirit who has been given to us."[Rom 5:5][63]

One can never put God in a box. God's Spirit animates all and prompts all to serve. It is in this service that Christians in a special way exercise their kingly role, a leadership role done in service to others. Ultimately this service is motivated by recognition of the great dignity of each and every human person. The human person's great dignity lies in sharing the same human nature that Christ Himself possessed and even now possesses.

Pastoral Care of the Family: Stages, Structures, Agents, and Situations

Stages of Pastoral Care of the Family

The Apostolic Exhortation, *Familiaris Consortio,* up to this point has spoken in very idealistic terms. In other words, in lived experience it is often hard to envision family life as described, however it is the ideal for which we are to strive. The Church is sensitive to her

---

62 John Paul II, Address at Mentorella Shrine (October 29, 1978): *Insegnamenti di Giovanni Paolo II,* I (1978), 78-79.

63 *Familiaris Consortio, ibid,* n. 63.

children in the complexities of life. This section attempts to deal with these situations. The document does call people to realize the impact a family can have and how the world will benefit if people attempt to live in reality the ideal that the Church puts forth.

This is to be accomplished by spiritual direction, pastoral care to all, and in particular to those who are experiencing difficult or irregular situations. These activities must be ongoing and not seen as merely for those in immediate crisis.

A natural focus lies in preparing people for marriage. It is important for people to realize the responsibilities of conjugal life but also where to turn when those inevitable times in life occur when trials and difficulties arise. In a culture that has and does reduce women and men to merely a means to gratify animal desires, appropriate values must be instilled. These values give insight into the true dignity of the human person. They also give one the means to recognize that a real intimate relationship between a man and woman is much, much more than what goes on behind bedroom doors. Sexuality must be perceived as a precious gift which is to be respected and offered to another in the context of a sacramental marital relationship, or it is to be withheld altogether for the kingdom of God in either religious life or priesthood. Many priests have had the opportunity to experience C.P.E. , *Clinical Pastoral Experience.* The encounters can be varied and certainly valuable. However sometimes people fail to respect one's tradition and practices. It seems that one of the goals is to elicit an emotional response from those engaged in the program. In one of the group sessions there was seemingly an attack on those who chose celibacy as their vocational choice. It was reported to me something like this, "Sex is so good, why would God ever ask anyone to forego the experience. This just seems like a ridiculous thing. If you had a Cadillac, don't you think God would want you to take it for a spin?" Again this comment was intended seemingly to get a reaction. I guess my answer to the question would go something like this, "If you had a Cadillac, would you have the generosity of spirit to keep it in perfect condition so that others could enjoy it in the future?" When celibacy is lived well, it enables the practitioner to be more available to God. One can deepen their spiritual life to such a degree in order to be a more effective instrument to help others.

Preparation for understanding human sexuality and its multifaceted gifts cannot be accomplished overnight. The *remote preparation* begins in early childhood; the *proximate preparation* involves teaching people the real value of the Church and what she offers to sustain and nurture her children.

This proximate preparation must include study of the nature of conjugal relations, responsible parenthood, with all the necessary medical and biological knowledge connected with it. In our sexually saturated, media driven society, it is not so obvious to many young people that monogamous relations are just good for the human family; and likewise promiscuous lifestyles weaken the human's immune system and make a profound and detrimental impact on the psychological health of the individual.

The *immediate preparation* for the celebration of the sacrament of marriage needs to take place in the weeks and months prior to the marriage.

Ongoing formation must take place after couples are married; particularly younger couples will often need help in coming to grips with the adaptation that is required in their new state of life and their new responsibilities with children. Older married couples should be resources for the younger couples. The church must help young couples realize the value of life and their obligation to serve life. This ongoing formation is available in the wonderful program called *Marriage Encounter*, a program that can be an excellent resource when its leaders are deeply rooted in the faith.

Structures of Family Pastoral Care

Priests and religious and laity need to be informed about medical, legal, social, or educational aspects that are important for helping families. It is important to engage married couples in such structures. Associations of families are also important to build support for living a vocation solely ordered towards sacrificial giving.

Agents of the Pastoral Care of the Family

Religious leaders have their obligations to guide people to form their consciences in a way that is amenable to the Gospel of Jesus Christ. Parents must truly guide their children and not let them fall prey to a mass media that is biased towards ideologies which run contrary to the true dignity of the human person. Attempts must be made to educate children in a correct understanding of the human person and his or her obligation to responsible exercise of his or her freedom. The media has an obligation to promote such responsibility and serve the truth.

> *In fact they (the producers of the media) are expected to avoid anything that could harm the family in its existence, its stability, its balance and its happiness. Every attack on the fundamental value of the family - meaning eroticism or violence, the defense of divorce or of antisocial attitudes among young people - is an attack on the true God of the human person.*[64]

Social communication is a powerful medium to form and guide peoples. All who really appreciate the true dignity of the human person are encouraged to enter this field and positively influence it. This is a daunting task in our world today as less and less respect seems to be apparent in appreciating the values of purity and normal family structures.

Pastoral Care of the Family in Difficult Cases

The Church is not in the business of judgment or condemnation. The Church is in the business of mercy and reconciliation. The Church's role is one of both mother and teacher. Some people find themselves in objectively difficult situations. The Church is called to respond with a shepherd's care.

The Church is to be a home for all, the migrants, the oppressed, all those who suffer. She must open her doors to all who wish to

---

64 Paul VI, Message for the Third Social communications Day: *AAS 61* (1969), 456.

enter. The Gospel parable of the king's banquet is helpful. All are invited; the individuals share some responsibility in getting ready for the feast. The Church is there to help people realize their obligations and will walk with them through the often difficult and trying times. It is sad when some fail to be open to such assistance. At the heart of the Church's response is it recognition of people's free will. Some make bad choices. The Church also emphasizes the need to respect the religious freedom of others. In other words the Church's mission is to propose the truth to all who will listen and impose it on no one! Many seem to fail to appreciate the distinction.

Irregular Situations

The Church offers clear guidance in many of the situations and circumstances in which many individuals find themselves. The first situation referred to is trial marriages. Though many see a value in such arrangements,

> ... *they are unacceptable, by showing the unconvincing nature of carrying out an "experiment" with human beings, whose dignity demands that they should be always and solely the term of a self-giving love without limitations of time or of any other circumstance.*[65]

The second situation would be *de facto free unions* (shacking up). Some people find themselves forced into such a situation for economic, cultural, or religious situations. Some would seemingly be exposed to harm if they contracted some formal arrangement. Others would opt for this arrangement to preserve "freedom" in a legal sense or merely as a convenient means to gratify their sexual needs. All of these situations are complex, so in dealing with such situations one must look at each carefully and gently guide those in these situations to help them regularize their situation, that being, guide them to an acceptable loving, life-long commitment in the Church.

For Catholics, a civil marriage is insufficient because of the implications of the sacramental union. In a civil ceremony, divorce

---

65 *Familiaris Consortio, ibid*, n. 80.

is always perceived to be an option. For a sacramental marriage, this cannot be an option.

Separated and divorced persons who have not remarried have not separated themselves from the Church. Only in the case when a person remarries is there a difficulty. Divorced persons who are not remarried need to be supported and encouraged to actively participate in the Church.

Divorced people who have remarried still need the support of the Church. However the Church can not extend an invitation to the Eucharistic Banquet. Again the Church is not trying to make an objective judgment on the state of their soul, but encouraging them to seriously consider the clear teaching of Jesus and His emphasis on the impossibility of divorce. In Matthew's gospel there is the "exception clause".

> *I say to you, whoever divorces his wife (unless the marriage is unlawful) and marries another commits adultery."* [NAB, Mt 19:9]

Sometimes the phrase in parentheses is translated "lewd conduct or adultery", the emphasis is clear that Marriage is something that is not to be taken lightly. The Church will honestly take a look at each situation so that if at all possible the relationship will survive. Clearly there are issues that endanger the spouse or children, and so it is not only morally permissible to separate, but there would be a moral obligation to remove oneself from a dangerous situation. The exception of an unlawful marriage is what the Church calls an annulment. This is when one of or both of the parties did not enter into the relationship freely or did not give full consent to the marriage free of conditions. Many people lack what is termed "due discretion" when entering into the marriage. From the beginning, one or both of the parties did not understand the demands of permanence or some psychological aspect could have prevented the person from being able to make such a commitment. Sometimes one of the parties is not open to life and does not reveal their true intentions from the beginning. Marriage is so important that the Church is willing to help couples more deeply understand its significance and importance for the human family to thrive. Any human who has experienced the pain of a divorce can understand why the Church strives to avoid such recourse at all costs. I personally believe that divorce is actually worse than death. I have seen couples survive after horrible betrayals. There is great joy when such forgiveness becomes manifest, when people choose to work out their differences and are able to be reconciled. The person who is wronged has a unique opportunity to reflect in a deep and profound way God's mercy. God's mercy is reflected in their own expression of mercy to the other. God will always take us back when we have failed, God invites us to show forth the same attitude.

In closing this chapter I think there is one important point to make. Indisputably, "The future of humanity passes by way of the family."[66] We must all, to the best of our abilities, strive to discover what the family is and how it can be lived in a way that promotes, protects, and preserves the dignity of the human person. No matter how corrupt, or how good a structure of society is, the individuals that make up that structure make all the difference in the world. For our part, it is better to try to positively influence those whom we touch than scream and cry out against structures that we can have little impact on. It may be appropriate to close this chapter with a somewhat famous prayer:

> *God, Grant me the means to change the things I can,*
> *The serenity to endure the things I cannot change,*
> *And the Wisdom to know the difference.*

---

[66]*ibid,* n. 86.

CHAPTER VII · EVIL IS *NOTHING* TO WORRY ABOUT!

I do not want the title of this chapter to be misleading. Evil is a reality with which to be reckoned. But evil is not "some thing", and it cannot be understood in terms of some material substance. No one or no thing is evil, but evil is that which has the capacity to destroy. Evil corrupts, distorts, perverts and is the reality that fuels deception. I think one of the great misfortunes of much of contemporary moral thinking is a real failure to grasp this. Not to get too heady, but a branch of philosophy that takes a look at what makes *something* what it is, is called ontology. The word *ontic* would signify the essence or "being" of some thing. Bear with me. I don't want to get carried away on some esoteric discussion; I think this topic is worth reflecting on to some degree. It will hopefully make some sense out of our situation today. If we consider some of the great insights that the great thinkers were able to come up with when reflecting on the *mysterium iniquitatis*, or the mystery of iniquity, or the mystery of evil, we will be able to deepen our own understanding of this self-destructive reality.

I know that common sense may not be so common, but if we simply try and apply a little logic, there is some sense that can be made out of life. The book of Genesis relates a story of how God created all this stuff, and when He made the stuff, it was all good. And in the end, all the stuff, and the pinnacle of the created order, the human person, was VERY GOOD. So if God is all good then where in hell (like the play on words) did evil come from? The solution to the philosophical problem is found as early as Augustine. Evil is not "some thing" but rather it is "no thing". Evil is a lack, a privation, something that is not what it should be! A person who cannot see is suffering from evil, in a sense. The eye is not working as it is intended to work. Cancer cells are cells gone mad. Sex outside of marriage sets up people for tremendous heartache, not to mention the tremendous instability for any child that may be conceived by such an illicit union. In the Christian tradition evil has no "being". Evil is the "no thing" we must worry about. Some contemporary moralists seem to want to co-opt the language and spill much ink on what they call "ontic" evil. In the traditional philosophical framework of Christianity this is truly the epitome of an oxymoron. At the heart of all evil is the perversion of some thing. Evil has no existence! I would suggest that this kind of thinking is the result of abandoning common sense. Back to the question, If a tree falls in the forest does it make a sound? Of course it does, even if no one is there to hear it. The bunny rabbit will jump, even if no one is there to see it.

In the first decade of the new millennium there was a superstar who had come under allegations of child abuse. In the past there were other allegations, but he apparently settled out of court. The sad irony of this case is that everybody knows that to treat a child in such a way is heinous, but the agonizing and devastating reality is that many of the perpetrators do not even think that what they are doing is wrong. According to many contemporary moralists, the moral quality of the act lies in the intention of the person alone. This is insane. If this superstar had taken some moral theology courses, he would be blameless and the moral act that he had committed would be a "moral good". This is madness, and I hope that all can agree with me. The sad thing is that contemporary moralists would argue that I do not understand, and yet they are the same people that want to legitimize sexual gratification with no openness to life and abortion in the "hard cases". Life must be the ultimate value if humanity is to survive. All life, and especially that which is most vulnerable, must be protected and preserved.

I spent some time in Nigeria with a native who lived with me for 3 years in the states. I was taken aback by the lack of infra-structure in the south of the country. Primarily this seemed to be the direct result of corruption. Even though by some accounts Nigeria is the third wealthiest country in Africa, its wealth is not transferred or shared with the people in any meaningful way. The most basic infrastructure seems to be lacking. It seems to be at the place the United States was in about 1700: plenty of natural resources, they simply needed a just system to enable those resources to be used for the benefit of the many. The road system was indescribable. It could take 5 or 10 minutes to even travel one mile on the roads. I had spent 10 weeks in Mexico, and as difficult as that situation was, there seemed to be some effort to have reasonable roads in the city.

Despite the severe material hardships in Nigeria, the people were very happy. They seemed to be a spiritually rich people. At a week day mass, a parish of about 5000 families would have attendance that ranged from 400 to 600 people! Some would come at 4 a.m. and pray in the form of Eucharistic Adoration and by the early mass at 5:30 am the church would be crowded.

Their devotion would confuse liberals and ultra-conservatives alike. There liturgies were lively and had moments of spontaneous prayer. For example, during the elevation of the host and the precious blood, the people in unison would say, "My Lord and My God!" Then when it came time for communion, they all approached the communion rail (contrary to popular belief, communion rails were not forbidden by the Church), knelt down and took communion on the tongue. They came with faith and no agendas ... what a deal that is!

Nigeria is a place with about 80 million people. I was told that unemployment was about 50%. One Nigerian man who was extremely kind asked me about abortion as a form of birth control. He put forth the scenario of a person with four children who can barely be fed, and a fifth just conceived. He seemed to think that abortion would be a viable option in such a case. After we talked for a time, and I had presented my side which sees people as always an asset and never a liability, he seemed to recognize that killing any human is never an acceptable solution. The sad reality that those in power often fail to recognize is that humans are the world's greatest natural resource. Only humans have the ability to solve problems.

It is true that we can create big ones too. But the bottom line is ultimately that we can make simple choices and make our world a better place without resorting to drugs, chemicals, or procedures that directly kill innocent human beings.

It is quite simple if you believe in God. If you don't believe in God then it is much harder to find real meaning and purpose in one's life. Since God is the master of life, as St. Anselm noted, that which is greater than that which cannot be thought, only He has the authority to directly take life. A person can freely offer his or her life to save another, but others may never make this decision for someone else. We must never destroy developing humans for the sake of a hoped for scientific break-through. Such choices are setting humanity up for destruction. If this value is not preserved, the concept popularized in the mini-series "Battlestar Galactica" may be closer than we think. If you are not familiar with that series, a set of robots sees how humans are not efficient and attempts to eradicate them by force to make a more efficient world. If all our technology is not ultimately aimed at serving humanity, all of it, then hope for humanity's future is waning. There is hope, and that hope is found in truth.

At the core of my priesthood is my desire to fight nothingness, and the best way to do that is to do something. George Weigal, in his 1999 biography on John Paul II, makes the excellent point that John Paul II seemed to have made the decision to combat the dissident theologians by presenting positive teachings on morality and the world. This approach was quite different from attacking dissidents and harshly treating those who are so confused. One thing that is very clear about the nature of evil is that it has a profound capacity to destroy itself. One needs only look at what a life of sin does to a person. Where would you like to start, drugs, alcohol, sex, pornography? These behaviors destroy families and individuals. They ultimately lead to unhappiness.

Again one of the fundamental characteristics of evil is its profound capacity to destroy itself. By its very nature it tends towards nothingness. I think one need look no farther than those in the Church who have been blinded by sin and committed heinous crimes against young people, particularly innocent children. These priests that have committed these vicious acts are often the same ones who have tried to legitimize their evil acts through such a misguided moral theology. The ultimate irony is that the media who champions such misguided views was the very instrument that has served to purify the Church from such erroneous teachings. Those in the media who saw this as an opportunity to attack the Church only served to purge a great deal of evil that was manifest in the midst of the Church.   In the parable about the weeds and the wheat there is something very striking about the vocabulary that the author of the gospel chooses to use. The word that was chosen to describe the weeds ζιζάνιον, darnel, or a specific kind of rye grass that can even be poisonous, looked much like the wheat until harvest time. The power of this analogy should be evident. Many who look the part of those who claim to be followers of Christ are often those that can choke off goodness. Under the guise of tolerance, rightly understood a very good thing, many will encourage behavior that is profoundly self-destructive. It looks good on the outside, but it is devastating to mental and physical health.

One need only to look at some of those priests who have been deposed and the teaching posts they held in the Church to see the damage that had been done. Consider how this was handled in the media. I really think that the media is a fairly neutral entity. It is populated by people who have been formed by a philosophy that seems to suggest that it is truth that is nothing at all, the kind of philosophy that makes the claim that a tree only makes a sound if someone is there to hear it! This philosophy lends itself to a misguided compassion, a misguided compassion that fails to recognize the absolute value of human life and that which is best to serve life.

I suspect that if you took a poll, most in the media would be more supportive of abortion and a much more relaxed sexual ethic. These are simply great evils. At the same time, the media proved to be instrumental in exposing the traitors among the ranks of the clergy who had not only sinned, but committed unspeakable crimes against the most vulnerable in our society. It is likely that the media was instrumental in cleansing the church of those misguided and deceived souls. These are likely the same souls who think more along the lines of the political and social values the media seem to embrace the most. Evil always and ultimately will collapse on it self. By its nature it is self-destructive. I am not one of those persons who thinks the media is a conspiratorial, evil institution bent on disseminating immorality every chance it gets! Nope, the media will present what it is fed. It is true that many in the media have been formed with values which I think are patently false, but many in the media have their heart in the right place.

In my own personal experience one Saturday afternoon, something that happened to me demonstrates the good will in the media. A gentleman who had been diagnosed with AIDS was obviously discouraged. He was drunk and came into the Church that was entrusted to my care. He used candlesticks like baseball bats, damaged statues, broke stained glass windows, threw condoms all over the Church sanctuary and even tried to pry open the tabernacle, the most sacred place in the Church. This is where Christ dwells in a real way under the appearance of bread. He was so drunk that he passed out on the floor. It made him easy to catch!

This was a huge media event for the local community. It was a Hispanic parish and the first question the media person asked was, "Do you believe this was racially motivated?" My immediate answer was no. The facts had not come out yet, but I had no reason to believe or jump to such conclusions. To make a long story short, the media followed the event. They even wanted to follow me to the local lockup when I visited the poor man. I declined such exposure. They also were kind enough to cover the re-consecration of the Church on the local news casts. They showed great compassion and concern. This event helped me to not characterize the media as an enemy but a valued friend that can indeed serve the truth.

For more proof regarding the neutrality of the media, one need look no farther than the coverage of the death of John Paul II. It was incredible. They were awed by the man and his inclusiveness. John Paul II seemed to see the face of Jesus in everyone he met. He recognized people's dignity, whether it was the unborn child or his assassin. He loved genuinely every human person and he cared for them. He knew that the Church had traitors in her ranks and apologized for their sin whether it be against the Jews or other Christian communities that were led to reform because of corrupt individuals and corrupt practices in the Church.

People are good, and everyone who knows oneself wants to do good. I believe it is St. Thomas Aquinas who states that we can only do the good. The difficulty lies in being fallible creatures who are easily deceived. When people make a choice it is not because they think it is evil, on the contrary they see it as a "good option". I think it is safe to say that all people both on the right and the left would be willing to see the institution of human slavery as evil. It seems obvious, how could anyone not recognize the dignity of a fellow human being? It is hard for the modern mind to conceive how any educated person would make such a value judgement based merely on the color of a person's skin. Yet it happened, and in some parts of the world it is still happening. Many today fail to grasp the dignity of a very young developing human, hopefully like slavery, such horrid abuse will become the thing of the past.

There was always the old saying that masturbation caused blindness. I have never seen such a thing written in any historical document, however it is written that sin causes us to become spiritually blind. Misusing the human body degrades our dignity. We are not simply one animal among many animals. Humans are called to rise above instinct and reveal a noble dimension of our being. The prohibition of masturbation fosters a sense of deep mastery, discipline and self control, sadly the teaching is often mocked. Again a beautifully clear teaching is successfully perverted in the minds of many. When we become consumed by "nothing" we will accomplish nothing. If a person wants to truly escape the grips of evil, they must become attracted to all that truly is some thing, namely all that is good.

To come to grips with evil is a very difficult thing. How does one try and go after "nothing"? Many people are very sick, and sickness is a kind of evil. The Church was often mocked by her strong emphasis on sexual purity and a well-ordered sexuality. The truth is that whenever we sin, no matter what the sin, we contribute to a real spiritual blindness. Sin really hurts our ability to see clearly in a spiritual way. I am convinced that Jesus knew what He was talking about when He used the image of the blind man leading others into a pit. It is the clear insight of the Church that will lead humanity out of its culture of death. As Augustine noted, it is crucial to know thyself. We must be willing to reflect on what the truth really is.

Many people seem so quick to believe that they posses the truth and that they cannot be mistaken. One of my early spiritual directors was quick to admit that he was spiritually directing people in the present, that he felt he had profoundly misled in his earlier days as a priest. It seemed that when he was young he was quick to question authority and failed to grasp the wisdom of the teaching of the Church. He seemed to be caught up with the mentality popularized by the book, I'm OK, You're OK by Thomas Harris in the 60's. My friend told me that he wanted to write a book, but he wanted to call it, I am not Ok, and You are not OK, and that is OK! The point being that there is something very wrong in the world. It is ultimately because of the human person's difficulty in knowing the truth and acting on that knowledge. We can overcome our weaknesses with God's grace. The real danger is when no one is able to recognize his or her lack of perfection. The truth is *something* with which to be reckoned. It is not only the hot button issues that have been co-opted for political gain, such as abortion and homosexuality, but true environmentalism must be open to an analysis that does not deny what is the truth.

A morality that is unable to recognize the objective aspects of moral acts is a useless morality. If one reflects for a moment, one realizes that if truth cannot be known, than any attempt at substantive communication is an exercise in futility. This misguided morality tends to place the moral value of the act as merely a result of personal judgement of the individual involved. It fails to make an incredibly important distinction, a distinction from the objective character of a particular moral act, and the personal culpability, or shall we say guilt worthiness, of the individual.

If God really is a good God, He only wants the absolute best for His creation. The natural order, when we truly come to understand it, allows the human person to do incredible things. We can build machines that fly, figure out drugs that treat symptoms and even sometimes cure natural defects. The moral plane is connected to this as well. When we determine the correct behavior, it serves our physical well being. We discover what foods are better for us than others. We learn how certain exercises can ease pain when done as physical therapy. Why is it so hard for people to realize that moral acts are healthy acts? They condition us to fully realize not only our physical potential, but out spiritual potential as well. Evil always is that lack of fullness that contributes to the human person's demise.

In the case of abortion, many in society fail to account for the emotional damage that the female incurs as the result of killing one of her own, and the emotional damage to the man that was equally responsible for the new life. Many fail as well to consider the far reaching societal damage that results from devaluing life. Even in simple and practical considerations the world is jeopardized by such evil acts. One can simply consider the fact of the diminishing labor pool and potential tax base for future generations. It should be self-evident that one of the reasons that social security is in such dire straits is the fact that since 1973 almost 1/3 of the new population has not been given a chance to live and thus pay taxes. If we fail to stop the evil now, it will really goof things up later. Ultimately it will stop itself later: evil by its nature is self-destructive. If any body can just sit back and think for a moment, he or she will be able to recognize the truth in the previous statement.

Many in our world are convinced that the end of the world is imminent. Many will point to the Bible's last book, the Apocalypse or the Book of Revelation. I truly believe that much of the Book of Revelation was fulfilled around 70 A.D. With that said, I do not mean to suggest for a moment that the book can have no future implications as well. I just find some commentator's analysis quite compelling. Many of the godless in our world today are destroying as many as one third of the population by abortion. According to the Guttmacker Institute 22% of pregnancies in the US ends in abortion.[67] This does not even count how many abortions are chemically induced by contraception or other forms of birth control that prevent the genetically complete human being from attaching to the uterine wall of the mother. Evil is seductive and can blind many from the reality of its damage. An interesting quote from the Book of Revelation should give everyone pause:

> *The rest of the human race, who were not killed by these*
> *plagues, did not repent of the works of their hands, to give*

67 http://www.guttmacher.org/pubs/fb_induced_abortion.html

up the worship of demons and idols made from gold, silver,
bronze, stone, and wood, which cannot see or hear or walk.
Nor did they repent of their murders, their magic potions,
their unchastity, or their robberies.[NAB Rev 9: 20-21]

It is important to note that the Greek word for "magic potions" is φαρμάκων, which is the ancient root for pharmaceuticals. It is not a reach to see this as chemical contraception.

Chapter VI spent some time on the issue of homosexuality, a psycho-sexual disorder. It is a kind of evil as are all disorders, such as blindness or any other physiological or psychological problem. I know that even placing homosexuality in such a category raises the ire of many, but until 1973 all the clinical manuals of psychology agreed with me. It can be plausibly argued that it was the strong lobby of gay activists and the corporations who sought to profit by not having to pay benefits for the treatment of the disorder that resulted in the successful reclassification of homosexuality. By saying this, it does not mean that homosexuals are evil. People cannot be evil, no one can be evil. We can do evil things, or we can be plagued by evil, but we are not evil. God only makes good stuff! Evil is self-destructive and damaging to the human person.

The goodness of the human person is at the root of the moral teachings of the Church. The Church loves people enough to tell them when they are doing things that are self-destructive or harmful to others. I can remember another conversation with a friend of mind who made it his life's work to serve kids who have lost their way. Often times they were in homes where they had been brought up in a context where they were given little worth and less opportunities to realize just how precious they were as human beings. Many had likely been abused physically and sexually. It is no wonder they struggle. I am still taken aback when people wonder why they act out in such hostile ways? This man was not a Catholic at the time, but was moved by the presumption of goodness of all people on the part of the Church. Prior to that time, he seemed to believe that religion viewed the human person as less than worthwhile and did not seem to value the intrinsic worth of the individual. It is understandable how he could draw such a conclusion. One early reformer viewed humanity as a "damned mass" that could only be covered over by the redemptive power of Christ. Humans, even those who do not respond to the gift of faith that is offered to them, are still intrinsically good. One needs to look no farther than Genesis chapter one to draw a conclusion of the profound and unique goodness of all of God's creation. We talked on various things for a couple of hours, and then months later, he showed up and wanted to come into the Church. Today he is a third order Benedictine. It was the value of the profound goodness of the human person that helped him to grasp the teachings of the Church of Jesus Christ.

Homosexual acts are wrong because those acts hurt the person who is deceived into living such a lifestyle. Like the alcoholic or drug addict, or those trapped by pornography, they are convinced that what they do is not hurting them. Anyone who has had to deal with alcoholism or drug addiction knows how hard it is for the one addicted to recognize the problem. Can you imagine how much more difficult it would be if society took the side of the alcoholic and denied natural law and said, "they are born that way, they cannot help it. Let them go! They are not hurting anyone but him or herself"? Here in lies the problem: do we care enough to try and help others recognize the truth as it is? It is hard and many will refuse the help, but just because people refuse to act in accord to what is best for them, it does not absolve society of the obligation to propose the truth to those who will listen. Evil is the perfection of isolation. There is no room for communal thinking in an evil regime. It is autocratic, and truth is determined by proclamation, not by insight into what is true for all. Law in its true nature is that principle that relates universally to the common good or physical properties.

Law is revised when it is shown to be in contradiction to that which is the truth. Laws can be passed that state that the sky is red from now on, but obviously that law is not a good law. That law would be patently false. If people believe that homosexuality is wrong because the bible says so, they are missing the point. The reason why the bible states that homosexuality is wrong is because it is bad for the human person and the society that exists. I realize that is a statement based on faith, but my faith is based on that which makes sense from a human standpoint as well.

The Church cares deeply and profoundly for sinners. If the alcoholic comes to me and confesses their sin, I have the great privilege of forgiving them on the authority given to me as the result of apostolic succession. If the alcoholic never approaches, I can never forgive him. How tragic it would be for him if no one cared enough to help him recognize his self-destructive behavior. Ultimately the demise of the human race will occur if the human person becomes so self-centered and he or she is unwilling to recognize that some things truly are wrong and detrimental to the human family. The individual will ultimately suffocate as the result of such isolation.

Environmental Issues

I am amazed at the polemics that exist on political fronts. Those on the left would have you believe that Republicans are set on poisoning the water supplies and polluting the air and in general just trashing the world. Facts are used on both sides that tend to over simplify incredibly complex situations. Here again, if we truly let ourselves be governed by what is true, we will be better served. The difficulty lies in discerning what is really the truth. One of the great benefits of being a priest is that one gets the opportunity to meet many incredibly interesting people. At a rehearsal dinner I was talking with a geologist. He informed me of the vast amount of oil that is being pumped into the ocean each day as the result of natural phenomena. Leaking fissures in the ocean floor, he claimed, far exceeds the amount of oil that resulted from the Exxon Valdese spill some years ago. Regarding Mount St. Helen's, I understand that objective scientific reports seem to suggest that the event was more damaging to the environment than all of man's efforts to pollute. By some estimates almost 1 million metric tons of CO_2 was released in the atmosphere by Mt. St. Helens. These natural phenomenon are serious problems, but the human person, as we grow in our understanding of the mechanisms of the world, are the only creatures on earth who have any hope of doing something about these problems.

We must, however, be aware that we can be mistaken. Fifty years ago they were convinced that the world was on its way to a new Ice Age. Good science is not at all in contradiction to true religion, but is mandated by it. In Genesis, the human person is given the command to conquer and subdue the earth. This obviously does not mean trash it. If we trash the earth, we will be destroying ourselves which again would go against the principles of true religion. I am utterly amazed that seemingly intelligent people place more value on a baby whale than a baby human. No baby whale will ever be able to solve an environmental problem. Until the whales start to compete in our universities or marketplace, it is just silly to see them on the plane of humans. We must respect life, all life. We must strive to understand the delicate balance of nature or we will ultimately destroy our planet, but my point is that we are called to be serious environmentalists, not to protect the animals, but to serve to protect the true balance of nature so that the human person can thrive. It really is all about the Human Person!

If we fail in our environmental efforts we may go they way of the Mayans. In one region in Mexico there is a place that currently is barren. In the past it was fertile and thriving. The inhabitants found they could work with wood more easily than stone. They cut down so many trees which served as shade to the natural cisterns, that the water stored in the ground evaporated too quickly and thus they lost their water supply. The settlement died. They died because they failed to understand the mechanisms of the environment around them. Sound environmentalism is concerned about the survival of man. It is inhuman to fail in our obligation to be good stewards of creation. Man is not the enemy of the world, man is the enemy of man. Man is the enemy when he embraces a lie instead of the truth. Evil is that *nothing* to worry about , it is this evil that foments war, hatred, confusion and the culture of death.

Chapter VIII · John Paul II on the Mystery of Human Suffering

Evil is that which truly is the cause of all suffering. Original Sin introduced this disorder into the world. John Paul II in his Apostolic Letter, *Salvifici Doloris*[68], sees suffering as bound up in the mystery of the human person. It is interesting to note that John Paul II wrote this Apostolic Letter after he had been shot and nearly lost his own life. The Holy Father addressed both contemporary and the traditional concerns. He extensively drew from the Sacred Scriptures; he referred to Holy Scriptures over one hundred times in a relatively brief document. This chapter will attempt to put forth the major tenets of the letter and assess how it addresses some of the issues which are of concern today. I truly believe his analysis is helpful in coming to grips with the large scale suffering which the person can sense in the world today; the oppression by corrupt regimes which is so prevalent today, innocent suffering, suffering surrounding death, and the suffering that is associated with those who are not distinct professing members of the Body of Christ, the Church.

The document, *Salvifici Doloris*, is divided into eight sections. The introduction and conclusion bracket six sections which look at various aspects of human suffering.

---

68 Pope John Paul II, *On the Christian Meaning of Human Suffering*, Vatican Translation, St. Paul Editions, 50 St. Paul's Ave., Boston, MA 02130.

The Introduction sets the tone for the entire letter by quoting the Apostle Paul, "In my flesh I complete what is lacking in Christ's afflictions for the sake of his body, which is the Church."[69] In the introduction it is posited that "what we express by the word "suffering" seems to be particularly essential to the nature of man." He suggests that it belongs to the human person's transcendence, something outside the individual. This is accomplished by putting a person in a situation in which he or she must face something which is mysterious, if not altogether unreasonable. John Paul II emphasized that it must be the Church's task to meet the human person in a special way on the path of suffering. Even though suffering remains an intangible mystery for JP II, suffering seems almost to be a necessary component to push the human heart to overcome fear. Suffering also provides us with something which only the imperative of faith can conquer.[70] Faith assists our ability to make sense out of things that are hard to grasp. It is clearly a mystery. My own father died when I was only 16. He was a good man who worked hard at being a good Christian. Why should the lives of such good witnesses be cut so short? These are difficult questions, faith merely interprets all things as working towards a greater good. This seems to suggest that faith is key in making the prospect of suffering to some degree coherent and bearable in human experience.

"The World of Human Suffering" is the next section. This part takes into account the human person's subjective experience, which cannot be transferred or expressed but "in its 'objective reality' [human suffering is] to be dealt with, meditated upon, and conceived as an explicit problem".[71] Human suffering cries out for a solution; at the very least it calls for the quest to seek answers. John Paul II pointed out that the Sacred Scriptures are a great account about human suffering. In many places, the Scriptures give us examples that bear the signs of suffering, especially moral suffering, loneliness and abandonment.

---

69 ibid, p. 5., n. 1.

70 *ibid*, p. 7., n. 4.

71 *ibid*, n. 5.

It is interesting to note that the Old Testament had no specific word to indicate suffering. Everything that was suffering was defined as evil. Only the Greek word πάκιω provides us with the distinction which no longer strictly identifies suffering with that which is objectively evil.[72] John Paul II suggests that suffering constitutes a specific "world" which exists together with the human person. This world provides the ground for solidarity among the human family. This is accomplished by the suffering that we all experience. By analogy it can help us, at least to some degree, relate with all those who suffer. The greatest examples of this phenomenon would be catastrophes and wars. These disasters can mysteriously bring people together in a way that may not be possible by any other means. This "world" shows forth unprecedented progress, and at the same time unprecedented danger due humanity's mistakes and offenses.[73]

"The Quest for an Answer to the Question of the Meaning of Suffering" is the third section of the letter. It is bound up in the nature of the human person to wonder, "Why?" Only the human person is aware of his or her suffering. Often times this can be used as the main and foremost reason to argue for the denial of God. The Pope uses Job to illustrate the point that not all suffering is the result of some fault. Though sometimes suffering is due to faults and transgressions, one cannot unequivocally accept that all suffering results from personal sin.[74] The book of Job can be seen as a foretelling of the sufferings of Christ, but in itself the story is sufficient to show the inadequacy of identifying suffering with moral order and the justice that transgressions seem to require. The book of Job asks the question, but provides no answer regarding innocent suffering.

John Paul II also noted that suffering seems to be used in the Old Testament as an invitation to mercy, to correct and lead the people to conversion. In one sense, human suffering exists for the sake of

---

72 *ibid*, pp.8_9, n. 7.

73 *ibid*, p.12, n. 8.

74 *ibid*, p.16, n. 11.

justice, but first and foremost it creates the possibility of rebuilding goodness in the one who suffers.[75]

These answers are still incomplete and not totally satisfying. The "why" can be most completely, though still not comprehensibly, addressed by the sublimity of divine love mysteriously manifested by the God-Man, Jesus Christ.

The next section, "Jesus Christ: Suffering Conquered by Love", addresses the mystery of this divine love as it relates to suffering. Jesus Christ is God's gift to humanity which provides the human person a means to escape definitive suffering, namely eternal damnation. This however is not the only suffering at which the mission of Christ is aimed. The Holy Father notes the complex involvement of sin with suffering, but emphasizes the fact that it is not always the result of someone's personal sin.[76]

The response of God to humanity's failure is His saving act in Christ. The motivation for this saving act is God's love for us. This is essential to giving some purpose to suffering in our concrete experience. In some mysterious way the "Lord has laid on him [Jesus] the iniquity of us all". [See Isaiah 53]

The Suffering Servant sections in Isaiah are seen as prophetic anticipations of the passion of Jesus. Jesus, like Job, carries the question with him, but unlike Job also carries the greatest possible answer. This answer is not only addressed by his teaching but also by his example of suffering.[77] The Pope seems to be suggesting that it is love that gives at least some coherence to suffering. The love is manifested most purely through obedience even amidst the great and ominous pains that Jesus freely embraced. Redemption is accomplished by the suffering that is associated with the cross. A component of this suffering, John Paul II states, is Christ's perception of the separation, and rejection by the Father that He experiences. This aspect of His suffering is due to Christ taking on sin and as St. Paul puts it, "made him to be sin who knew no

---

75 *ibid*, p.17, n. 12.

76 *ibid*, p.21, n. 15.

77 *ibid*, p.27, n. 18.

sin".[78] The main point of this section is that the "cross of Christ has become a source from which flow rivers of living water". It is through this cross that suffering can be given at least some degree of coherence or intelligibility.

The fifth section is titled, "Sharers in the Suffering of Christ." John Paul II again reflected upon the Song of the Suffering Servant in Isaiah. This poetic text foreshadows what the cross of Christ will accomplish, namely that all human suffering finds itself in a new context or situation as a result of the passion of Christ. John Paul II's radical idea of incarnation is clearly reflected by the statement,

> *Every man has his own share in the Redemption. Each one
> is also called to share in that suffering through which the
> Redemption was accomplished.*[79]

Even though this does not give us the reason for suffering, it does let us know that we suffer in solidarity with Jesus Christ. John Paul II really emphasizes the redemptive value of human suffering. The dignity of the human person is such that suffering for truth and a just cause point to the human person's greatness.[80] The Pope makes it clear that one who is not explicitly Christian still shares this dignity implicitly.

Suffering is in fact always a trial. The Pope notes that interpreting suffering as was done in the past is not without merit. Suffering as in Job is a trial, but it also provides a means to be spiritually formed. He again comes back to Paul's image that personal sufferings complete the afflictions lacking in Christ's own sufferings.

The Church in her own way sees the good in redemptive suffering, and is called to give reverence to it and the mysterious Body of Christ that is within herself.[81] The people of God share in the mystery of human suffering. The Pope seems to be suggesting that this sharing

78 *ibid*, p.28, n. 18.

79 *ibid*, p.30, n. 19.

80 *ibid*, p.35, n. 22.

81 *ibid*, p.39, n. 24.

is not without its gifts. <u>Suffering cannot be thought of as something altogether evil</u>.

"The Gospel of Suffering" is the next section in the Apostolic Letter. This *Gospel of Suffering* was and is written by the Redeemer Himself. This Gospel is a living Gospel which continues to be written down by those who suffer persecutions for Christ's sake. As history unfolds, so does the Gospel of Suffering. This Gospel includes those who suffer for Christ and those who are suffering with Him here and now and in the future.[82]

It seems that John Paul II placed suffering at the very heart of human existence. Suffering causes one, seemingly almost by nature, to question "why". In this questioning one can recognize that one suffers in solidarity with the individuals who experience the torment and anguish of human suffering. Clearly this insight can only come slowly, but when it comes the human person can find within one's own suffering interior peace and even spiritual joy![83] It is very important to realize that suffering, though mysterious, is not without its positive value. All the Church, all the suffering brothers and sisters, is a multiple subject of Christ's supernatural power. All the members of the Body of Christ contribute unceasingly to the composition of the *Gospel of Suffering*.[84]

The next Section is" The Good Samaritan". The Pope uses this story to illustrate what it truly means to be a neighbor in the Gospel of Suffering. In a way suffering exists in the world to unleash love in the human person. This story not only speaks of something deeply Christian, it also reveals something universally human. Society, even divorced from Christian ethics, recognizes the intrinsic goodness about the charity that the story conveys. John Paul II states how important it is to relate, through the vehicle of education, the right attitudes. One must get a sense that one is called personally to bear <u>witness to love</u> in suffering.[85] The human heart needs to be touched!

82 *ibid*, p.43, n. 26.

83 *ibid*, p.46, n. 26.

84 *ibid*, p.47, n. 27.

85 *ibid*, p.52, n. 29.

The pope also emphasizes that this sensitivity to the salvific meaning of suffering is in no way to be seen as passivity. The Gospel is the negation of passivity in the face of suffering.[86] Since it is the negation of passivity it calls for judgment. It is quite clear that if we do not respond to the suffering of humanity, we stifle love and we stifle our ability to recognize the One Who is Love. We are called; Jesus taught "man to do good by his suffering and to do good to those who suffer". John Paul II stated that Christ has fully revealed the meaning of suffering in this double aspect.[87]

The document concludes by suggesting that suffering is at once both supernatural and human. The supernatural aspects stem from the divine mystery of the Redemption, and deeply human because only the subject discovers oneself, one's own humanity, one's own dignity, and one's own mission. Suffering is part of the mystery of the human person. The mystery of the human person is particularly impenetrable, but in the light of the Incarnate Word it can make some sense. The pope quotes *Guadium et Spes* which seems quite appropriate here, "Through Christ and in Christ, the riddles of sorrow and death grow meaningful."[88]

I think the document really helps us grapple with the complex issues that the world faces today. The question is, "Does this document speak today to all peoples; those who seem to be innocent victims, those under structures of injustice, those who face deep loss at death, those who do not experience suffering with the light of Christ?" These are difficult questions, and more than I can adequately address in this short chapter. I would maintain that the document is keenly sensitive to these issues.

Innocent suffering, as all suffering, largely lies in the realm of the incomprehensible. If it shows us anything, it opens our eyes to the fact that suffering is more than just a result of personal sin. Pastorally this is a very important message to convey. One can never say that suffering is always the result of "one's" own sins. John Paul

---

86 *ibid*, p.52, n. 30.

87 *ibid*, p.54, n. 30.

88 *ibid*, p.55, n. 31.

II emphasized the point by the story of Job. The innocent do suffer, though mysteriously, human suffering is not without merit. I would argue that he deeply appreciated the innocent sufferer is placed in union with Christ's redemptive suffering. The innocent sufferer is not alone. Christ, who was the paradigm of innocence, suffered first and continues to suffer in the members of His Body, the Church. This aspect places the sufferer in solidarity with all those who suffer, especially the spotless Lamb, Jesus Christ. Even though we may never be able to totally comprehend why, we at least know that we are never alone. This may sound abstract, but it seems to be true if we look at those in the tradition who so identified themselves with Christ that they could not help but suffer. This dimension of the truth about suffering may not take the physical pain away, but it at least gives purpose to suffering. Human suffering understood in such terms may even in some sense be the condition which provides the possibility for experiencing the joy that John Paul II mentions.

The Pope recognized the need for the human family to try and liberate people from suffering when possible. He seemed to be sensitive to the concerns of Liberation Theology. He made the distinction between definitive suffering, eternal damnation, and that suffering which is experienced in our earthly life. Christ conquered the power of definitive suffering. The suffering that we experience now is so intrinsic to the nature of the human person that it is not without its positive aspects. Even though there is something deeply human about trying to alleviate human suffering, it is the definitive suffering from which we will be hopefully liberated. The Pope is clear that the Christian has a real sense of responsibility to alleviate suffering where he or she can. The story of the Good Samaritan is the perfect example of this responsibility taken seriously.

The positive meaning of human suffering is mysteriously manifested in light of the cross and resurrection of Jesus Christ. Death, that final bout with human suffering, is conquered through Christ. If suffering is seen as something unjust and useless it will move the person close to despair. If, on the other hand, one can see it as sharing in the redemption of the world, then even the suffering of death brings us to the destination that we all await.

Human suffering is something that all people face. Some face it for the sake of justice and truth. It is clear that those who suffer for justice and truth, even though they are unaware of the Christ event, manifest a deep goodness that resides in the human person. The Pope recognizes that this heroic response is only possible because of the great dignity of the human person.

In concluding this chapter I think that there are two points throughout this Apostolic Letter that makes it so important today. The first concerns the centrality which John Paul places on the mysterious aspect of suffering being at the very heart of the nature and dignity of the human person. And the second relates to the vicarious nature of human suffering.

John Paul II notes the positive dimensions of the mystery of human suffering. Even though suffering has resulted from Original Sin, God has redeemed human suffering by the Christ event. Suffering opens up awesome potentialities for the human person. Human Suffering can be used as an instrument for the most brutal, inhumane behavior. At the same time human suffering provides the means for a person to show great compassion and love. It is Christ's example in the face of suffering that shows us the real dignity of the human person.

The vicarious nature is exemplified by the image John Paul II draws from St. Paul, the image that relates to making up for the sufferings that lack in Christ's afflictions. As difficult as it may be to try and help people understand this mystery, especially amidst grievous suffering, it is imperative for making some sense out of suffering. The human family's ultimate solidarity lies within the person of Christ. Jesus prayed that "all be one, as you, Father, are in me and I in you."[89] As this is so, the Gospel of Suffering continues to be written each day we live and breathe.

---

89 John 17:21, NAB.

Chapter IX · Good is *Something* to Believe In!

In some circles they talk of the transcendentals. Generally speaking these are things that are not easy to define. A theologian, Johannes Baptist Lotz suggests that there are four "transcendentals", namely: unity, truth, goodness and beauty[90]. These things all contribute to the essential characteristics of all that we experience. There is something incredibly awesome when all these aspects come together. When people feel united, from the married couple to the nation, it leads to a deeper understanding of what actually is the truth. From this unity, true goodness is evident and clearly, then, a person is able to experience beauty in its perfect form. We need only to look into our own experiences to recognize these various aspects of our personal lives. This chapter will be a reflection on some of my own personal experiences that have revealed true unity, truth, goodness and beauty to me.

John Paul II's writings have been an inspiration to me on many levels. I believe he truly loved everyone and was tremendously compassionate in many respects. The best biography to date in my opinion on the life of John Paul II is George Weigal's work, <u>Witness to Hope</u>. I think it is clear if one looks at the way John Paul

---

90 Johannes Baptist Lotz, *Transcendentals*, <u>Encyclopedia of Theology, The Concise Sacramentum Mundi</u>, edited by Karl Rahner, p. 1746, Seabury Press, New York, 1975.

approached things, that he spent much more time striving to build structures that were good, than trying to quell dissent or silence dissident theologians, or to put it another way, those traitors among the ranks. Only when theologians questioned the most basic tenants of the faith, such as the bodily resurrection of Jesus, or those that would deny the virgin birth, were disciplinary action taken against them.

It is evident that people have a general sense of what is good. As mentioned earlier St. Thomas said that the human person is designed to only be able to do the good. The problem is that we can be deceived and choose something that is evil, but we believe to be good. The sad fact is that people often exchange a lie for the truth. The Church will never deny that which is good

I can remember one of my first pastoral assignments. I was only a young seminarian at the time. The pastor received a call from a young woman who wanted to come back to Church. The pastor thought I could handle this one. I talked to this young woman on the phone and she related how her father told her that his obligation was to get her confirmed, and after that it was her choice. So after she was confirmed, she decided to quit going to church. I explained to her that it was very simple to return to the Church; she needed only to receive sacramental confession and she could return to the practice of her faith. She still said she wanted to talk to me. She came and during the appointment she related the same events concerning confirmation and her father's plan. She added that when she would return to the church for a wedding or a baptism there seemed to be some sense, or feeling that was unique in the Church. She seemed to express a certain uneasiness. I simply repeated that all that was needed was to return to sacramental confession.

As I recall the exchange she stated, "Hey, I am living with a guy, and if I thought it was wrong, I would not be doing it!" I simply agreed with her, and then posed the following questions or concepts, "This relationship that you have with this man, does it take sacrifice? Do you have to swallow a lot?" She immediately agreed that she did have to put up with a lot. I pointed out that any meaningful relationship will take sacrifice on our part; the same would apply to a meaningful relationship with God.

I then followed up with a story that just came to mind. It went something like this. Imagine that an engineer designed a machine for a certain community and the community frequently used the machine. After a while the machine was not working very well. The people were getting angry as if they had been cheated or had been sold an inferior piece of equipment. Finally they complained to the designer. The designer asked if they had been following the instructions? They responded, "what instructions?" When they found the instructions and put them into practice, the machine began to function well again.

The woman spontaneously burst into tears and said something like, "I guess I should live a celibate lifestyle until I am married!" I certainly agreed but the story does not end there. I was young and I had just informed this person's conscience in what I considered to be a gentle way. This whole encounter led to an interesting reflection, and even some complaints to God. It is always a challenge to prick one's conscience and I always try and be clear enough and at the same time gentle in helping people recognize objectively sinful behavior. That afternoon I remember posing some questions to God myself. My thoughts basically seemed to challenge God, some thing like, "God, you expect a lot out of us. I mean, I never saw the Red Sea split in two and I have never witnessed any columns of smoke, let alone the resurrection! Aren't you expecting an awful lot from us Lord?" I went so far as to say, "How can you possibly understand how hard it is for us to believe this stuff? Then it hit me like a ton of bricks..... Jesus.... Jesus must have known what it was like. After all, the scriptures tell us he grew in wisdom. These were my thoughts.

Just as a point of speculation, the scriptures state that Jesus was like us in all things. Faith is part and parcel of the human experience. John Paul II in *Fides et Ratio* discusses how the knowledge one acquires by faith is a distinctive knowledge, one that is more certain than any scientific proof. This event caused me to speculate about the relationship between Mary and Jesus. After all, as the story goes, Mary's faith brought her to her fiat, her "be it done to me according to your word", this amidst the uncertainty of being killed for having a child out of wedlock. I believe at the time Capitol punishment was the penalty for premarital-sex under strict Jewish observance. So after the angelic encounter and her experience of pregnancy I find it interesting that, in a way, she needed to have no faith concerning the Child in her womb. This Child was from God; this was evident from the angel's message. So as Jesus grew, in one sense, the scriptures report that he grew in wisdom as well as in strength. It seems that there must have been a conversation at some point that went something like this. Who knows, it may have occurred just prior to Jesus' trip to the temple. Mary said, "Jesus, uh... you see that guy Joseph over there, well, uh, you see, uh, well your father and I never had relations like other parents. You see, this angel asked if I would bear a Son, and I said yes and boom, nine months later we have God's son. That would be you!" Jesus may have responded in utter amazement, "Come on, what you are saying?" Mary may have pointed him to the suffering servant in Isaiah, or instructed Him to search the scriptures, and ultimately He knew He was the guy, but He knew it through human faith, just like all of us who have to come to believe through human faith. As I said He was like us in all things but sin. We really can identify with Jesus; I believe He made us that way.

This story illustrates in a very clear way our intrinsic ability to know the good and long for it. We can know the good if we just take the time to reflect on the implications of our actions. The good is always connected with life and its value. This intrinsic goodness is ultimately humanity's only hope. We see in children both profound innocence and profound selfishness. At the same time it is evident that children learn racial hatred and bigotry. Our society feeds self-centeredness, but at the same time we see the benefits of choosing the good and avoiding evil. The good choices we make strengthen our spirit. Honestly, when we do something difficult, like visiting someone in a desperate situation, a nursing home or cancer, do we not feel like we truly used our time well? We see this in the tremendous outpouring of volunteer organizations and the desire for many to improve desperate situations either home or abroad. We need to look no farther than the recent outpouring of support for the victims of Katrina and the other global disasters.

I recall a presentation given by a parent about the faith and how to nurture it in family life. She suggested that what many call the interior life begins for the child when the child first says "thank you". This is the first time that the little human values the presence of another human. This is a profound step in self-awareness and one's relation to another.

There was a recent study done on the attitudes of youth and religion. One salient point was that most youth thought religion had no serious impact on the state of "happiness". It did not matter if you asked a religious youth or one that practiced no specific faith. This was the consensus of opinion, but the facts played out quite differently. Those who were religious had lives marked by purpose and productivity and were far less likely to get into trouble with law enforcement agencies or be trapped by destructive relationships or behaviors.[91] The Truth will always lead to a more fruitful and productive life.

Another one of my favorite images concerns two young people in love. (This is a very good thing by the way!) The young woman says to her boyfriend, "Could you drive up to the upper peninsula of Michigan and pick up my sister? I know there is eight inches of snow on the ground and another foot on the way, but it would be such a big help!" The young man, at the prospect of spending a little time with his girlfriend, is overjoyed and thrilled to be trusted to do such a thing. Well the four hour drive turned into an eight hour drive and all the while the young man is happy and just filled with joy to be with the one he loves. If they marry, ten years later they will probably look back and say, "boy was that stupid". But at the moment, love makes those things which seem so difficult, very easy. Doing the good is always easy when we are truly motivated by love.

A fundamental aspect of our nature, our anthropological core, is our innate ability to be givers. I often suggest the following little reflection to demonstrate the point. I suspect there has been a time when you have looked long and hard for that special gift for someone you cared about, a father, mother or spouse or friend. You think you found the perfect gift and your feeling is confirmed by the incredible reaction of the one who received the gift. How does that make you

---

91 Soul Searching, The Religious and Spiritual Lives of American Teenagers, Smith, Christian, with Melind Lundquist Denton, Oxford University Press, 2005.

feel inside? Now turn the story around only this time you are the recipient of the gift. It is certainly nice to receive nice gifts, but honestly, is not the deeper joy found in the giving? For most people this is clearly evident. For those who have been abused or brought up in a highly dysfunctional environment it may be different, but generally I think this is the way we are meant to be!

Another pastoral situation that I have had is the varying response by those who humbly recognize the Church's invitations to her teachings and those who obstinately refuse them. I have a custom at funerals and weddings to explain the Church's understanding regarding the reception of communion. There are many who believe that communion is a beautiful symbol that can be an effective instrument of unity. In other words, there should be an "open" invitation to all who would desire to partake, baptized or not; just so long as one had a desire to "commune" with us, that is enough for them. The Church's teaching sees the Eucharist as the effect of unity. In other words, when unity is truly present, then and only then should one take communion. This is the position that will truly foster unity and help us to be driven to communicate and truly understand one another. My statement at the liturgies is succinct, but clear. It is something like this:

> *When we take communion in the Catholic Church we are saying that we believe in everything the Catholic Church, holds, teaches and professes to be true. For that reason the Church feels she has no right to impose that obligation of belief on those who are not Catholic and those who may have chosen not to practice their faith.*

Depending on how mixed the crowd is, I point to the passage in Corinthians that states that those who take this without understanding actually are harmed by it. Paul uses the strong language of condemnation! Nonetheless I will often invite those who cannot partake of the Eucharist to make a spiritual communion with our Lord and Savior Jesus Christ. I have received overwhelming support for this approach, and I have raised the ire of others. Seemingly the vast minority find it offensive.

I have found that many people have been living with burdens that were the result of bad information. On more than one occasion I have had people attack me and say, in effect, "I was divorced and you are saying I cannot go to communion!" They failed to realize that divorce was not the issue, but that entering into another marriage without the blessing of the Church is what would keep them from receiving communion with the appropriate disposition. I vividly remember one angry person who said, "I am going to communion", effectively saying, "I don't care what the Church says!" In reality she had not remarried and had been opposing a Church teaching in her mind, which was not the Church teaching at all!

Certainly there are many people who are married and divorced in the pews who have been given council to just go to communion any way, it doesn't matter. "God understands!" This bad and incorrect advice is given instead of encouraging them to approach the proper channels and initiate the annulment process, a process that can be a profound opportunity for healing and self-discovery.

I have known people who have made some poor choices in their lives and now find themselves in irregular marital situations. But their response has been quite the opposite of obstinate resistance. On the contrary, they have availed themselves to the annulment process and have patiently waited for the judgement of the Church, all the while refraining from the Eucharist until such a time as they can receive Him after the marriage has been validated in the Church. Some are seemingly so resolved that if the judgment should not go in their favor, they would make a spiritual communion until their circumstances change.

I have personally witnessed incredible fidelity amidst these difficult situations. I have known people who have been very involved with the life of the Church and patiently endured their situation. The document on the family written by John Paul II addresses such situations and does it in a way that is respectful of those who find themselves in difficult situations and is respectful of the challenging standards set forth by the Church.

I truly am at a loss when it comes to reflecting on what makes it click, what is it that moves the disposition of the human soul in such a way that people are open to belief and trust in Christ and

His Church? Once the openness is there and a person is willing to investigate the faith, things will then begin to fall into place. As mentioned before, if we truly accept things as they appear to be, it gives us an advantage. If we really accept the fact that a rock sinks, we are more likely to discover the reasons and physics of buoyancy, as opposed to trying to discover why rocks float. To make a direct correlation, if we wonder why the Church is correct, we will get much farther in our understanding, than if we assume that the Church is obviously in error. If we test Church teachings against unity, truth, and love, we will discover the beauty of the Church's teaching and the marvels of the Mystical Body of Christ. We will discover the *Splendor of Truth*. Again John Paul II reflects on the splendor of truth in another encyclical. He is a man that is personally inspiring to me, and I think his writings are worth reading and reflecting upon.

Chapter X · John Paul II and the Splendor of Truth · The Ultimate Good

I honestly feel that I have always had a passion for the truth and I find that John Paul II has a special gift in shedding light on deep realities that give hope to humanity's future. I really think it is extremely valuable to reflect on his work, *Veritatis Splendor*.

This Document, *Veritatis Splendor*, is addressed to the Bishops of the Roman Catholic Church. Its language can be difficult, but its purpose is to reflect on foundations that Catholic Moral thought is based and built on. The fundamental assumption is that Truth is that which liberates as opposed to something that enslaves or somehow limits freedom.

> *Truth enlightens man's intelligence and shapes his freedom, leading him to know and love the Lord*[92]

The document begins in expressing faith in Jesus Christ, faith that Jesus is the "true light that enlightens everyone". From the beginning, Catholicism has accepted a world view that is rooted in experience, and has recognized man's ability to grasp at least partially the transcendent character of truth: in other words, that aspect of

---

92 John Paul II, *Veritatis Splendor*, St. Paul Books & Media, 50 St. Paul Avenue, Boston, MA 02130, 1993, p. 9.

the truth that is not dependant on the human person. From our first parents there is an innate tendency to believe that the individual is the ultimate source of truth. The Church attests to the fact that even she in not the master of truth, she is truth's steward, its faith filled steward, living and enduring because of the commission given her by Christ Himself. She recognizes the human person's tendency to exchange the truth for a lie.

> *Man's capacity to know the truth is also darkened, and his will to submit to it is weakened. Thus, giving himself over to relativism and skepticism (cf. Jn 18:38) he goes off in search of an illusory freedom apart from truth itself.*[93]

This language can almost sound reactionary, or unrealistic. What is relativism or skepticism? Maybe you have heard it said, "***That may be all right for you, but I have my truth and it is not the same as your truth!***" Or, "in *the name of being 'sensitive' one should not impose one's views on another.*" In our culture, such language is taken for granted. These are seen as truisms, in other words, that which taken to be obviously the truth. The implication would be the query, "*How could anyone hold another opinion in a world that is based on freedom and rights?*"

The document, *Veritatis Splendor,* cuts to the heart of the debate. Are those statements above really true? Let us digress for a moment. I was a part time chaplain at a *Catholic* high school and in a class I was discussing aspects of religious freedom. The Church clearly teaches in the Vatican II document on Religious Freedom[94] that one cannot use coercion or force to compel one to "believe". I proceeded to say that those who are not blessed with faith in Jesus Christ our not necessarily doomed to eternal damnation, but rather simply mistaken. Truth does not depend on our perception. It has a transcendent character; in other words, it goes beyond the individual. Our faith as Christians demands that we love even those who fail to embrace the

---

93 *ibid*, n. 1, p.10.

94 *Dignitatis humanae*, Vatican Council II The conciliar and Post conciliar documents, Editor: Austin Flannery, December 7, 1965, pp. 799-812.

truth of Christ. One student became indignant with this response and said that such a position was arrogant. She posed, "how can you say that?" I responded with the question, "which is more arrogant, to believe in something that has endured for thousands of years (e.g. the Judaic-Christian tradition) or to suppose that the human person in his or her lived experience of a few years or even a few decades is the source and only reliable avenue to know the truth?" This student did a wonderful thing she posed a question. It is through the questions that we gain insight. I think it is important to ponder such things. I would contest that much of our problem today is the result of people not reflecting on important issues.

We as humans cannot escape asking questions. Why do we suffer? Why is there hatred? Why is there racism? Why do people have such little regard for the environment? Ultimately we raise the more fundamental questions.

> *No one can escape from the fundamental questions: What must I do? How do I distinguish good from evil? The answer is only possible thanks to the splendor of the truth which shines forth deep within the human spirit, as the Psalmist bears witness: " There are many who say: 'O that we might see some good! Let the light of your face shine on us, O Lord'"(Ps 4:6)[95]*

I really believe that ultimate meaning can only be found in Jesus Christ. The world's academics have accepted a politically correct agnosticism. Token religious liberties are assumed and couched in language of rights, but this freedom is not necessarily rooted in any concrete ability to recognize the objective truth relating to human dignity, but rather only understood as preserving the human person's license to be master of his or her own destiny. An important question one should pose is, "what is my *faith?*" Is it a faith in an understanding of freedom that is equated with license to do anything? Or is it rooted in the real as something that does not depend on the human person's perception? Catholic faith leads to the proclamation of Jesus

---

95 John Paul II, *Veritatis Splendor*, St. Paul Books & Media, 50 St. Paul Avenue, Boston, MA 02130, 1993, n. 2, p. 10.

Christ and true insight into the depths of the mystery of the human person:

> *Christ is "the way, the truth, and the life (Jn 1:14). Consequently the decisive answer to every one of man's questions, his religious and moral questions in particular, is given by Jesus Christ, or rather is Jesus Christ himself, ..."In fact, it is only in the mystery of the Word incarnate that light is shed on the mystery of man. [Gaudium et Spes, n. 22]*[96]

The Church believes that she is an "expert in humanity". Unlike other religious institutions that may boast of ancient roots, the Church alone has always sought to "convert" the world by engaging with the world. The Church is an expert because she has always recognized that she must be in the world but not of the world. She learns as the ages plod on. The Church "places herself at the service of every individual and of the whole world". [*Gaudium et Spes n. 16*][97]

The direct purpose of this encyclical is aimed at affirming the Church's moral teaching. It sometimes uses technical language that makes it difficult to understand for those not up on the lingo. Some main thrusts are to point out the weakness of some theological perspectives that seem to detach "human freedom from its essential and constitutive relationship to truth".[98] Also the questions are posed: Do the commandments of God, which are written on the human heart and are part of the Covenant, really have the capacity to clarify the daily decisions of individuals and entire societies? Is it possible to obey God and thus love God and neighbor, without respecting these commandments in all circumstances? Answers to these questions have been put forth that seem to be irreconcilable with the Gospel of Christ. This encyclical is intended to give guidance to some present day tendencies that don't have foundations in the Gospel of Christ and His Church. In other words, some contemporary proposals

---

96 *ibid*, n. 2, pp. 10-11.

97 *ibid*, n. 3, p. 11.

98 *ibid*, n. 4, p. 13.

are not founded on truthful principles and fail to respect human dignity.

Some of the assertions may be bold, and certainly not "politically correct", but maybe, just maybe *they might be true!* As you continue through this chapter I challenge you to work through it with an open mind. I believe that if you search your heart and open your mind you will be compelled to believe and have deeper insight into the splendor of truth!

It might be worth restating Pascal's Gamble at this point. If there is a God, then if we obey his commands (e.g. make finite sacrifices: refrain from sex outside of marriage, don't cheat or steal, treat all with respect and be honest, etc.) then we stand to gain something that is infinite: eternal life with God and His heavenly Hosts - *an infinite gain.* If there is no God and we make these finite sacrifices we still will avoid sexually transmitted diseases such as AIDS, and stay out of prison. We may lose some finite amount of pleasure, but we die and there is nothing, we rot and decay and enter into an eternal cycle of meaninglessness - *only a finite loss.* But, however, if we choose to deny the reality of God and we solely let our beastly appetites be our ruler, we may gain some finite amount of pleasure, but the consequences will be eternal damnation with Lucifer and his fallen angels - *an infinite loss.* It would seem as though even pagans should take those odds.

The remaining part of the document, *Veritatis Splendor,* is broken down into three chapters, the first begins by reflecting on the story of the rich young man in Matthew's Gospel 19:16. The second relates to the vocation of the Christian to be in the world, but not conformed to it, from Romans 12:2. The third section deals with the Power of the Cross, 1 Corinthians 1:17. Let us now turn to a reflection on the rich young man.

"Teacher, What Good Must I Do...?" (Mt 19:16)

The rich young man asks Jesus the question, and Jesus' first response was, "obey the commandments". The young man pursues the issue," what do I still lack?" Perfection Jesus says lies in selling your possessions and giving the money to the poor.

Veritatis Splendor points out that whether the young man knew it or not he was asking the morality question. The "*question* is not so much about rules to be followed, but *about the full meaning of life*".[99] This question is the most important question that the human heart can ask. Before the question can even be posed the person must be somewhat reflective. Today it is difficult to create a space to be reflective, but we too must pose the same question to Christ.

> People today need to turn to Christ once again in order to receive from Him the answer to their questions about what is good and what is evil. Christ is the Teacher, the Risen One who has life in Himself and who is always present in his Church and in the world.[100]

It is really hard today to believe that Christ is really that present, especially in anything as complex and as big as the Church. The church is understood as the People of God. Those who are its people are those who do the things Christ did and does through members of His Body. No human being can claim that they have such insight into anyone's true membership into this body. Truth is that which unites people to Christ, whether the individual fully recognizes it or not. One of the most profound mysteries, if not the most profound is the mystery of the Incarnation, an Incarnation that reaches across the ages; the buzz word would be *trans-historical*. This is probably not how we have understood it, but it is the essence of what it means to be truly human.

> "*The man who wishes to understand himself thoroughly - and not just in accordance with immediate, partial, often superficial, and even illusory standards and measures of his being - must, with his unrest, uncertainty and even his weakness and sinfulness, with his life and death, draw near to Christ. He must, so to speak, enter him with all his own self; he must 'appropriate' and assimilate the whole of the*

---

99 *ibid*, n. 7, p. 17.

100 *ibid*, n. 8, p. 18.

reality of the Incarnation and Redemption in order to find himself. If this profound process takes place within him, he then bears fruit not only of adoration of God but also of deeper wonder at himself.[101]

This idea of the Incarnation is absolutely necessary to make sense out of so much of Catholic teaching. Be it the aspects of *inpersona Christi*, (e.g. the priest at mass and in confession is actually "in the person of Christ while he administers the sacraments), or the teacher, health-care worker, or anyone who consciously becomes aware of their need to be Christ for one another through service. There is that wonderful story about Mother Theresa, who being followed by a reporter, was tending to a dying gangrenous man. The stench was overbearing from the decaying flesh. She picked him up in her arms and was taking him to a place where he might die with dignity, love and concern. The reporter is to have been so repulsed by the man that he stated, "I wouldn't do that for a million dollars!" Mother Theresa simply replied, "Neither would I!" It was her understanding of the Incarnation that led her and leads her followers to serve the poorest of the poor. For they believe, along with me, that they are serving and tending to the needs of Christ Himself. "Whatsoever you do to the least of my brothers and sisters, you do unto me!" (Mt. 25:40)

The rich young man called Jesus, "good teacher". Jesus asks the question, "Why do you ask me about what is good? There is only one who is good. If you wish to enter into life, keep the commandments". The document points out that it is God and God alone who can answer the question about what is good, because he is the Good itself.

Obviously there is a faith component here. Where are the moorings? What are we connected to? God gives us His Word, His commands, His Spirit. This Spirit enlivens the Church and has dwelt with His Church from the beginning. The Church's sole purpose is to be the Body of Christ which is in intimate communion with the Father and the Holy Spirit.

---

101 *ibid*, n. 8, Quoting the Encyclical Letter, *Redemptor Hominis* (March 4, 1979), p. 18.

The Church, instructed by the Teacher's words, believes that man, made in the image of the Creator, redeemed by the Blood of Christ and made holy by the presence of the Holy Spirit, has as the ultimate purpose of his life to live "for the praise of God's glory"[102]

What is the Moral life? The word morality comes from the Latin, while the word ethics is derived from the Greek. They are equivalent terms, both relating to what is done, action and behavior: the science of determining right from wrong.

A contemporary journalist recounted an experience he had. He was suggesting that the moral decay in society had something to do with the way values are presented. He was arguing that the Judaeo-Christian Values should serve as a basis. A student took issue with his position and the journalist asked for a counter proposal. The student had none. He asked the student what she had been studying in school and what year she was in. She said that she was a senior and was taking Ethics as a major. How amazing: after four years of study, she could not even come up with an intelligible suggestion. When we are conditioned to believe that we can only answer our own questions, it will be impossible to come up with any plausible counter proposals. In other words, the only rule is that there can be no rules. This statement in itself is not logical. It fails to satisfy. Forty years ago abortion was seen as a heinous war crime perpetrated by the Nazis. Today many mistakenly see it simply as a choice rooted in a right to privacy. In another 40 years will rape be reclassified, or incest, or bestiality, or sex with children? Already the paraphilia - homosexuality - is touted as just another means to express one's sexuality. Could not the argument extend to pedophilia? No reasonable human being would accept such reasoning. Fifty years ago no reasonable human being would deny the right to life of an unborn or preborn child! "Truth, what is the Truth?" Pontius Pilate's words ring out today resoundingly! Morality must be rooted in something, what is it?

---

102 *ibid*, n. 10, p. 20.

The moral life presents itself as the response due to the many gratuitous initiatives taken by God out of love for man. It is a response of love, according to the statement made in Deuteronomy about the fundamental commandment: "Hear, O Israel: The Lord our God is one Lord and you shall love the Lord your God with all your heart, and with all your soul, and with all your might. And these words which I command you this day shall be upon your heart; and you shall teach them diligently to your children (Dt. 6:4-7)[103].

The rich young man was given the command, "Obey the commandments!" Do we believe that God created things and made them good, and not to be a waste? What does believing entail? Practically, what should our response be? Who will tell us what to do? The faith filled response begins with the commandments. The commandments are significant: Jesus Himself links them to the promise of eternal life "If you wish to enter eternal life, keep the commandments". (Mt 19:17)

I remember helping in a confirmation program at Purdue when I was a student there. I hope I will never forget one girl's response when asked why she was in the program. She said with deep emotion and tears welling up from within, "I want to be a child of the light". To be a child of the light we must begin by obeying God's commandments. This is the first step. The commandments are integral:

The Ten Commandments are part of God's Revelation. At the same time, they teach us man's true humanity. they shed light on the essential duties, and so indirectly on the fundamental rights, inherent in the nature of the human person.[n 2070] .... They are the first necessary step on the journey towards freedom, its starting point, "the beginning of freedom, " St. Augustine writes, "is to be free from crimes .. such as murder, adultery, fornication, theft, fraud, sacrilege and so forth. Once one

---

103 John Paul II, *Veritatis Splendor*, St. Paul Books & Media, 50 St. Paul Avenue, Boston, MA 02130, 1993, n. 10, p. 21.

> *is without these crimes (and every Christian should be without them), one begins to lift up one's head toward freedom. But this is only the beginning of freedom, not perfect freedom...*[104]

One of the main concerns of this document is to clearly describe what true freedom is, freedom not seen as merely license but rather being free to become who we are called to be: children of the light.

The fullest expression of the new law is the Sermon on the Mount. This sermon contains the fullest and most complete formulation of the New Law (cf. Mt 5-7), and is clearly linked to the Decalogue (the Ten Commandments) entrusted by God to Moses on Mount Sinai.

> *In the "Sermon on the Mount," the magna charta of Gospel morality, Jesus says: "Do not think I have come to abolish the Law and the Prophets; I have come not to abolish them but to fulfill them" (Mt. 5:17).*[105]

Jesus, in emphasizing the law of God, does not put neighbor before the love of God, but unites them as something integrally bound together.

> *Jesus brings God's commandments to fulfillment, particularly the commandment of love of neighbor, by interiorizing their demands and by bringing out their fullest meaning. Love of neighbor springs from a loving heart which, precisely because it loves, is ready to live out the loftiest challenges. Jesus shows that the commandments must not be understood as a minimum limit not to be gone beyond, but rather as a path involving a moral and spiritual journey towards perfection, at the heart of which is love (cf. Col 3:14)*[106]

---

104 *ibid,* the document quotes [*In Iohannis Evangelium Tractatus,* 41, 10: CCL 36, 363 , n. 13, p. 25.

105 *ibid,* n. 15, p. 26.

106 *ibid,* n. 15, p. 27.

This reflects a more stringent command to live purely and lovingly and not contribute to the culture of death that is so prevalent.

Perfection lies in something much deeper than mere adherence to precepts. When the rich young man pursues Jesus and asks the question, "What more can I do?" Jesus' response invites the rich young man to do something quite radical, to *freely* give his possessions to the poor and follow Him. Jesus' invitation was prefaced with the words, "If you wish to be perfect". This story of the rich young man is used to emphasize the fundamental link between freedom and God's law.

> *"If you wish..." These words of Jesus reveal the particular dynamic of freedom's growth towards maturity, and at the same time they bear witness to the fundamental relationship between freedom and divine law. Human freedom and God's law are not in opposition; on the contrary, they appeal one to the other. The follower of Christ knows that his vocation is to freedom. "You were called to freedom, brethren" (Gal 5:13), proclaims the Apostle Paul with joy and pride. But he immediately adds: "only do not use your freedom as an opportunity for the flesh, but through love be servants of one another"[107]*

The document, citing Augustine, relates that conflict found within, between true freedom and slavery. Practically speaking, if someone attacks you physically or verbally, the temptation is always there to lash out against the aggressor. Are we free when we give into such responses? The person of virtue is free to respond in a constructive way that can be more or less blunt, while the person enslaved will often spew out venom that can wound relationships and cause a breakdown in communication. In us all there is probably that dimension of freedom and slavery. The task is to be drawn towards freedom, to become freer and freer, to become more human, as Jesus is human, to truly be ourselves, the self that God created, to be a lover, a lover of God and a lover of neighbor.

---

107 *ibid*, n. 17, p. 30.

To respond to Jesus we must follow Him:

> *This is not a matter only of disposing oneself to hear a teaching and obediently accepting a commandment. More radically, it involves holding fast to the very person of Jesus, partaking of his life and his destiny, sharing in his free and loving obedience to the will of the Father. By responding in faith and following the one who is Incarnate Wisdom, the disciple of Jesus truly becomes a disciple of God (cf. Jn 6:45).[108]*

The mystery of the Incarnation is at the heart of what it means to be a disciple. It is not simply imitating actions or the things that Jesus did. We must do that, but the key is to be "conformed" to Christ.

> *Following Christ is not an outward imitation, since it touches man at the very depths of his being. Being a follower of Christ means becoming conformed to him who became a servant even to giving himself on the Cross (cf. Phil 2:5-8). Christ dwells by faith in the heart of the believer (cf. Eph 3:17), and thus the disciple is conformed to the Lord. This is the effect of grace, of the active presence of the Holy Spirit in us.*
>
> *Having become one with Christ, the Christian becomes a member of his Body, which is the Church (cf. 1 Cor 12:13, 27)[109]*

Jesus does not mince words with the rich young man. In fact, the man left "sorrowful, for he had many possessions" (Mt. 19:22). The disciples themselves were taken aback and they were dismayed. *Veritatis Splendor* quotes the passage:

> *But the Master refers them to God's power: "With men*

---

108 *ibid*, n. 19, pp. 32-33.

109 *ibid*, n. 21, p. 34.

this is impossible, but with God all things are possible"
(Mt. 19:26)[110]

This relates to how hard it was to give up things even then. Today we have so much more competing for our attention. TV and radio glorify sex and make it out to be a game. Nothing is left to the imagination. It is interesting to note that immediately after Jesus' encounter with the rich young man, Jesus talks about marriage and its indissolubility (it cannot end),that marriage is for all of life. Radical freedom is being able to not be possessed by anything or any one. Jesus himself noted, "Not everyone can accept this saying, but only those to whom it is given" (Mt 19:11) Remember that this radical call again is impossible for man, but can be lived out by the grace of God. The human person "becomes capable of this love only by the virtue of a gift received".[111]

This whole conversation between the disciples and Jesus raises some interesting questions about the relationship between law and grace. It is through grace that we possess true freedom, freedom to fulfill the law.

> *The gift does not lessen but reinforces the moral demands of love: "This is his commandment, that we should believe in the name of his Son Jesus Christ and love one another just as he has commanded us" (1 JN 3:32) One can abide in love only by keeping the commandments, as Jesus states: "If you keep my commandments, you will abide in my love, just as I have kept my Father's commandments and abide in his love" (Jn 15:10).*

Love is the answer, but what does that concretely mean? How can we interpret this reality? In today's world, instead of asking the question of interpretation, society's faith has assumed solely a personalistic approach to the interpretation of moral questions. The question of *meaning* arises. What is the source of meaning?

---

110 *ibid*, n. 22, p. 35.

111 *ibid*, n. 22, p. 36.

Meaning comes from God and God alone. If there is not a creator, I find it impossible to come up with any real purpose to life, other than be strong and try and kill others before they kill you. There is an anecdote that G.K Chesterton would carry a gun and when he would encounter people who subscribed to such a hopeless philosophy, he would volunteer to end their life; needless to say he found few takers. Our faith teaches us that Christ is God, and God dwelt among us in Jesus, Jesus is the Teacher, and thus gives meaning to life, even if our life is marked by suffering it indeed has purpose. We are never alone:

> *The Teacher who expounds God's commandments, who invites others to follow him and gives the grace for a new life, is always present and at work in our midst, as he himself promised: "Lo, I am with you always, to the close of the age" (Mt 28:20). Christ's relevance for people of all times is shown forth in his body, which is the Church.*

The Church speaks from a faith perspective that she can interpret the moral law only because of the gift given her by Christ. Today many would question the place of the church's Magisterium in teaching, but the council affirms,

> *"the task of authentically interpreting the word of God, whether in its written form or in that of Tradition, has been entrusted only to those charged with the Church's living Magisterium, whose authority is exercised in the name of Jesus Christ."*[112]

A fundamental purpose of this document, *Veritatis Splendor*, is to help clarify the Church's living tradition so as to assist, guide and direct some of the tendencies of contemporary moral theology. The Church begins from fidelity to Jesus and the tradition of the Church. The church's task is to "help man in his journey towards truth and freedom".

---

112 *ibid,* (within the quotations is taken from *Dei Verbum* n. 8), n. 27, p. 41.

The next section of the document begins with the phrase, "Do Not Be Conformed to This World". (Rom 12:2) The Church envisions her vocation as not one who is master of the truth, but merely a faithful steward of the truth as it has been revealed through Jesus Christ.

> *The Church has faithfully preserved what the word of God teaches, not only about truths which must be believed but also about moral action, action pleasing to God (cf. 1Th 4:1); she has achieved a doctrinal development analogous to that which has taken place in the realm of the truths of faith. Assisted by the Holy Spirit who leads her into all the truth (cf. Jn 16:13), the church has not ceased nor can she ever cease, to contemplate the "mystery of the Word Incarnate," in whom "light is shed on the mystery of man."*[113]

The Church challenges society's conventions. In other words, the Church adheres to the Gospel and not to what society perceives in any epoch to be "moral". In Paul's second letter to the Thessalonians verse 2:15, it states, "Therefore, brothers, stand firm and hold fast to the traditions that you were taught, either by an oral statement or by a letter of ours."[NAB] The Church submits to the authority of the scriptures, the traditions taught by "letter", but she is also, because of her fidelity to the scriptures, faithful to those traditions passed on by "word". The Church understands this to be the apostolic tradition passed on through the apostles to the bishops throughout human history. This today would be understood to be the Magisterium of the Church. The Magisterium is the bishops throughout the world. We believe as Catholics that the teaching office, the Pope along with his bishops who relate those things consistent with the Church's teaching of the past, is truly guided by the Holy Spirit. Many take issue with this today. History can be a very good teacher.

The abuses of humanity that were occurring in the New World were addressed. As early as 1537 the Papal bull, Sublimis Deus of Paul III denounced those who held that "the inhabitants of the West Indies and the southern continents...should be treated like irrational animals and used exclusively for our profit and our service." The pope

---

113 *ibid*, n. 28, pp. 43-44.

solemnly affirmed that: "In the desire to remedy the evil which has been caused, We hereby decide and declare that the said Indians, as well as any other peoples which Christianity will come to know in the future, must not be deprived of their freedom and their possessions-regardless of contrary allegations-even if they are not Christians and that, on the contrary, they must be left to enjoy their freedom and their possessions"[114]

The historical evidence affirms the teaching that the Church is indeed an expert in humanity, though the message is difficult to relate. Many will choose to ignore the facts. The facts are there to support the Church's perspective.

The Church is not master of the truth. It cannot whimsically change specific teachings that culturally may seem inconvenient, whether those teachings be the enslavement of another human being or abortion or even contraceptive techniques that take away and make impossible the open free and total gift of one spouse to another. The truth does not depend on us or our perceptions. The truth is the truth. It is in this fundamental insight that the Church has lost any semblance of political correctness.

The Second Vatican council encouraged a renewal in perspectives. The new perspectives were aimed at deepening and making more understandable the truths to which the Church has faithfully submitted, the truths that are sometimes, only with great difficulty, expressed in such a way in which they can be understood. *Veritatis Splendor* tries to clarify and correct those who have lost sight of the Church's faith. The Church's intent, as it has been throughout all of history, is to champion deeper insight into the mystery of Christ while calling to accountability those who lose their way and faith in the Church's guidance.

> *The work of many theologians who found support in the Council's encouragement has already borne fruit in interesting and helpful reflections about the truths of faith to be believed and applied in life,......the Church, and*

114 *The Church and Racism*, The Pontifical Commission Peace and Justice, November 3, 1988, Published by the Daughters of St. Paul, 50 St. Paul's Avenue, Boston, MA, n. 3, p.11.

particularly the Bishops, to whom Jesus Christ primarily entrusted the ministry of teaching, are deeply appreciative of this work, and encourage theologians to continue their efforts, inspired by that profound and authentic "fear of the Lord, which is the beginning of wisdom"(cf. Pv 1:7)

At the same time, however, within the context of the teological debates which followed the Council, there have developed certain interpretations of Christian morality which are not consistent with "sound teaching"(2 Tim 4:3)[115]

The word "teological" refers to arguments that are principally concerned with the *ends* and do not necessarily become preoccupied with considering the *means*. In other words, some contemporary approaches are concerned with the consequences (or ends) of an act (e.g. consequentialism). Others concern themselves with determining the proportion of "good or evil". This difficulty stems from being able to draw lines and make good judgments.

Veritatis Splendor lays out some fundamental "principles necessary for discerning what is contrary to "sound doctrine," drawing attention to those elements which seem to be confused or misunderstood. A fundamental principal relates to the quality of an action. Freedom is exercised accordingly when the good is chosen. Whenever one directly chooses to do something that is in itself or intrinsically disordered, one abuses true freedom. Today the concept of freedom seems to be at the heart of the debate. The Church respects freedom and in particular exalts religious freedom.

---

115 John Paul II, *Veritatis Splendor*, St. Paul Books & Media, 50 St. Paul Avenue, Boston, MA 02130, 1993, n. 29, p. 45.

> *... in particular, the right to religious freedom and to respect for conscience on its journey towards the truth is increasingly perceived as the foundation of the cumulative rights of the person.*[116]

This freedom is somehow confused often with an understanding that freedom is license and has no transcendent connection with truth as it is.

> *Certain currents of modern thought have gone so far as to exalt freedom to such an extent that it becomes an absolute, which would then be the source of values. This is the direction taken by doctrines which have lost the sense of the transcendent or which are explicitly atheistic. The individual conscience is accorded the status of a supreme tribunal of moral judgment which hands down categorical and infallible decisions about good and evil. .... But in this way the inescapable claims of truth disappear, yielding their place to a criterion of sincerity, authenticity and being at peace with oneself," so much so that some have come to adopt a radically subjectivistic conception of moral judgment.*[117]

Truth is not something that is unknowable or something that does not relate to anyone but the individual.

> *Once the idea of a universal truth about the good, knowable by human reason, is lost, inevitably the notion of conscience also changes. Conscience is no longer considered in its primordial reality as an act of a person's intelligence, the function of which is to apply the universal knowledge of the good in a specific situation and thus to express a judgment about the right conduct to be chosen here and now.*[118]

---

116 *ibid*, n. 31, p.47

117 *ibid*, n. 32, p. 48.

118 *ibid*.

The problem today is that people fail to recognize the significance and binding nature of universal and fundamental truths. Either Jesus Christ was the Son of God or he was not. You may freely choose what you would like to believe, but your belief has nothing to do with the reality of Jesus Christ as a Divine person. The document moves into a discussion of law and its relationship to freedom. If God exists, and theologians certainly operate from this context, there are certain implications of such a belief.

> *God's law does not reduce, much less do away with human freedom; rather, it protects and promotes that freedom. In contrast, however, some present-day cultural tendencies have given rise to several currents of thought in ethics which center upon an alleged conflict between freedom and law. These doctrines would grant to individuals or social groups the right to determine what is good or evil. Human freedom would thus be able to "create values" and would enjoy a primacy over truth, to the point that truth itself would be considered a creation of freedom.*[119]

The document proceeds to explain why this approach is unsatisfactory. We can recognize that freedom cannot be without limits. Who could ever hold that rape could be a good exercise of someone's freedom? Today the world is so confused that killing is reduced to simply a choice a woman should have when it comes to abortion. Our culture has made many mistakes in the past as noted with regards to slavery, and more recently the holocaust. We as God's creatures are not the *creators* of values; this cannot be. We must attempt to form our conscience in such a way that it conforms not to the world of darkness, but rather to the world of light, the world of Truth.

> *The relationship between man's freedom and God's law is most deeply lived out in the "heart" of the person, in his moral conscience. As the Second Vatican Council observed: "in the depths of his conscience man detects a law which he*

---

119 *ibid*, n. 35, p. 51.

*does not impose on himself, but which holds him to obedience.
Always summoning him to love good and avoid evil ... To
obey it is the very dignity of man; according to it he will be
judged (cf. Rom 2:14-16) [Gaudium et Spes, n. 16]*[120]

The conscience is sovereign, but not infallible. We must confront ourselves with the question, "Who is my master?" The way we answer that question will determine the way we will strive to live. We must follow our conscience but we must also strive to form our conscience in accord with the truth.

Another debate that the document addresses is that of "Fundamental Choice". This is that which also has been termed the "Fundamental Option". In concept, it relates to our fundamental orientation to either the good or the bad. This "fundamental choice" shapes our life. The importance of this choice is obvious, but this fundamental choice can never be seen as somehow distinct from concrete particular actions. Contrary to some contemporary tendencies to get away from the distinction between mortal and venial sins, the document points to the importance of keeping such a distinction.

*Reflection on the fundamental option has also led some theologians
to undertake a basic revision of the traditional distinction between
mortal sins and venial sins. They insist that the opposition to
God's law which causes the loss of sanctifying grace - and eternal
damnation, when one dies in such a state of sin - could only be the
result of an act which engages the person in his totality: in other
words, an act of fundamental option.*[121]

Clearly the church states that she has always maintained the importance of such a distinction.

*For Mortal sin exists also when a person knowingly and willingly,
for whatever reason, chooses something gravely disordered. In
fact, such a choice already includes contempt for the divine law, a*

---

120 *ibid*, n. 54, p. 72-73.

121 *ibid*, n. 69, p. 88.

rejection of God's love for humanity and the whole of creation; The person turns away from God and loses charity. Consequently, the fundamental orientation can be radically changed by particular acts.[122]

The moral act that could merit damnation must include the following conditions: a personal must have an informed conscience that acts with full knowledge, reasonable reflection, and full consent of the person's will to complete the immoral act. I would argue that many today suffer from a kind of invincible ignorance that puts forth concepts that are false and damaging. A person, before being held accountable before God, must have the intention to reject God and His commands. It is with such an attitude can one be threatened with eternal damnation. The document takes seriously the question, "Is the person morally responsible? At the same time, because of the very nature of truth, we can make judgments about concrete actions. And believers must never do evil so that good may come about. Among the approaches that the document calls into question, there is a certain lack in the ability to make clear judgments about certain behavior. These faulty approaches try and qualify an act as something without intrinsic moral content. These systems try to make judgments solely based on the perceived proportion of good or evil. They basically, in a nuanced way, are advocating that the end justifies the means. To put it simply the document states that it can never be right to do what is wrong! These approaches are not viable because truth is relegated to the realm of something subjective and having no transcendent implications. A quote near the end of the document places the ability to recognize the nature of the moral act intrinsically connected to the true dignity of the human person.

By acknowledging and teaching the existence of intrinsic evil in given human acts, the Church remains faithful to the integral truth about man; she thus respects and promotes man in his dignity and vocation. Consequently, she must reject the theories set forth above, which contradict this truth.[123]

---

122 *ibid*, n. 70, p. 89.

The final section in *Veritatis Splendor* opens with the quote, "Lest the Cross of Christ be emptied of its Power".(1 Cor 1:17) The fundamental question concerns the relationship between freedom and truth.

> *According to Christian faith and the Church's teaching, "only the freedom which submits to the Truth leads the human person to his true good. The good of the person is to be in the Truth and to do the Truth."*

A person, through human freedom, has the option to see oneself as sole arbiter:

> *Man comes to realize that his freedom is in some mysterious way inclined to betray this openness to the True and the Good, and that all too often he actually prefers to choose finite, limited and ephemeral goods. What is more, within his errors and negative decisions, man glimpses the source of a deep rebellion, which leads him to reject the Truth and the good in order to set himself up as an absolute principle unto himself: "you will be like God" (Gen 3:5)*

When a person comes to know the truth, then and only then will the truth set him or her free. Sadly, even some Christians by and large live as though there is no God that gives guidance. Humans are easily deceived and do things that truly are harmful to themselves. Many fail to recognize what is truly for their own good and the good of others around them.

Faith can guide us to the truth, if our faith is directed to that which is true. Faith in something that is directed to something false can be devastating. Walking in the light is much easier than walking in the dark. It is easy to fall and trip over things that are not visible. Faith illuminates our path in a big way, and the truth of the cross is monumental in coming to grips with reality:

---

123 *ibid*, n. 83, p. 104.

Jesus then is the living, personal summation of perfect freedom in total obedience to the will of God. His crucified flesh fully reveals the unbreakable bond between freedom and truth, just as His resurrection from the dead is the supreme exaltation of the fruitfulness and saving power of a freedom lived out in truth.[124]

The document, *Veritatis Splendor,* points to the reality that in today's world there is an attempt to place freedom and truth in opposition to each other. This is a grave error. This in turn feeds another dangerous dichotomy that separates faith from morality. Faith is more than just a set of propositions.

Rather, faith is a lived knowledge of Christ, a living remembrance of His commandments, and a truth to be lived out.[125]

To be a priest is to be a servant of the truth. There is indeed a splendor to such truth. When we encounter the truth, we cannot help but be changed. The truth makes an impact on us. When we reject the truth we do it to our own peril. If we are willing and open to the truth, then we also have every reason to hope that we will find it. To know the truth is humanity's only real hope at survival.

---

124 *ibid.*n. 87, p. 109.

125 *ibid.*n. 88, pp. 110-111.

Chapter XI · Humanity's Hope · Human Dignity and Religious Liberty

The first question one needs to ask, if this chapter is going to make any sense is, "Does the individual or human person have value?" How you answer that question will determine if there is a realistic hope for humanity's future! From a purely secular perspective it would seem plausible that every human person should be able to accept a simple, basic observation that seems to be self-evident. Namely, we are smarter than the beasts! It is this simple! This may seem hard for some to take, but humans are smarter than their pets. After all, the pets are owned by their "owners". Dogs and cats have not organized a "revolution" to be freed from the oppression of the pet owners. In fact, most pets seem to be quite content with their owners.

We must combat the pervading culture of death. This culture of death can be understood as a culture that fails to recognize the great dignity of the human person, in other words, humanity's goodness. It fails to grasp the singular importance of human life; yes, HUMAN life. Humans are quite different than all other creatures in that we have seemingly a much greater capacity to reason. Humans also feel emotion on a much deeper level than any other species on earth.

It should be clear by now that I do believe that every human being is important, and literally we all are equally important. Certainly there are differences in our abilities and the functions we can perform, but that must never be confused with the intrinsic worth of each person. A person may make decisions in their own lives to benefit others, but others must never make judgments to "take out" others for the benefit of the whole. Let me use a real life example. It is tragic, but it points to that deep and natural instinct to value others before oneself. I met this person when she was a little girl. I was friends with her sister when I was in high school. This little girl grew up to be a mother of twins. One day she was innocently crossing the street pushing her double stroller, when a driver, who sadly was distracted, was making a turn and failed to recognize the pedestrian traffic. When the driver finally looked directly in front of her, she saw the mother, and in a panic, is believed to have hit the gas instead of the brake. The mother instinctively shoved the stroller in front of her, and the children were spared. However she died. A mother's instinct to protect her children points to our inner most tendencies. We have a instinct to value others. This comes naturally to a mother. For the Christian, this ability to value life extends to every human being on the planet. Think of how quickly the world's problems could be addressed if we put such a priority on each human being!

I am astounded at some contemporary views and what is judged as important by many. It certainly isn't the individual. These same persons who hold these contemporary views, e.g. abortion, euthanasia, embryonic stem cell research, seem to be the ones making the allegations opposing the Church and attacking her teachings! One need only reflect on the premise of Dan Brown's popular novel, The DaVinci Code. He seems to suggest that the Catholic Church is bent on suppressing the "divine feminine". The most tragic aspect of the book's popularity relates to the number of people who give credence to his "fictional" proposals. In my own pastoral encounters I found it hard to believe how many people made serious inquiries about aspects of the book. I was actually taken aback when the book seemed to "reveal" the pinnacle of practice, or what it held to be the essence of communing with the divine. It seemed to suggest that this was accomplished in a voyeuristic sex act accompanied by chanting minions who were "entrusted" with the secret of the future blood line. The conspiratorial allegations of the book are such a far reach from credible historical sources that are available. Dan Brown goes so far as to suggest that before the emperor Constantine (~300 AD) Jesus' divinity was an open question. This is truly and simply ridiculous. Christians were killed for their faith in the divinity of Christ. Even though persecutions were not sustained or all that frequent by some historical accounts in the Roman Empire (a kind of an almost seemingly don't ask, don't tell policy), nonetheless Christians lost their lives over their faith in the divinity of Christ. Any student of ancient history knows well that these persecutions dated as early as Nero in the first century and other emperors up to the time of Constantine who lived in the fourth century. Many, many people are duped by the blatant denial of historical fact. This is what gives totalitarian regimes their sway. It is believed that Goebbels, one of Hitler's henchmen, said something to the effect, "Tell a lie often and long enough and they will believe it!" It is just so sad to me that so many attack the Church without even knowing what the Church teaches. We need to look no farther than the corrupt political regimes of the past to see the truth of such things.

I am somewhat amazed at the popularity of Dan Brown's book. By some estimates it is the best selling novel of all time. The book seems to champion old Gnostic or even occult ideas that were long ago dismissed as patently false. It seem tragically ironic that the "divine feminine" he seems to champion sees women as merely an object to be used. It strikes me as interesting how little character development is found regarding the woman that is used in the seemingly occult rite to further the blood line in his book! It is sad that the sex act is reduced to something mechanical and impersonal.

In the period that Brown seems to idealize, women were often nothing more than temple prostitutes to be used. These so called "suppressed" religions of the Divine Feminine were tremendously oppressive to women and saw them often as merely an object for sex and instruments of pleasure.

Human dignity is at the heart of what the Church is all about. Because the Church is the Mystical Body of Christ, the blood of Christ pulses through every member of His Mystical Body, not merely one cultic blood line. The scripture says that Jesus could raise up the very stones to be related to Him; He certainly would not have to resort to voyeuristic sex acts to pass on His blood line. It really is laughable. If one truly wants to understand the true beauty of sexual relations, one needs look no farther than John Paul II's Theology of the Body. If God is God and He created us (I know that this is a leap of faith, but I also believe it to be a fact), then every dimension of who we are as humans points to who God is.

John Paul II's understanding related in the early papal audiences of his pontificate, even develops the meaning of sexual relations. Sexual relations are to be a full and conscious gift of oneself to the other. These relations can only reflect the majesty and infinite potential of God when the act is open to life! Love is true when it is selfless. I think there was a popular song that had the lyrics, "What does love have to do with it?" The answer is simple, "nothing when there is no openness to life!" Chastity and self-control equip the human person to be in a position to make a more complete gift of oneself to the other. Masturbation is not only a sin because it misuses the sexual faculties, but it also sets people up to see others as an object to be used as opposed to a person to be loved. God wants married couples to experience the fullness of the joy and pleasure that God intended for them.

Man and Woman are distinctly complementary. One cannot understand in any meaningful way what it means to be human with out understanding the full dimensions of both masculinity and femininity. God is neither exclusively Masculine nor Feminine (Jesus being the exception in the Incarnation), but God's presence is revealed in the various aspects and attributes of both man and woman. Sigmund Freud's anthropology is extremely male dominated and biased in comparison to the insights offered by John Paul II.

Love is truly at the heart of Human Dignity and every dimension of the human person. God is Love and God created us in His image so it makes sense that love is key in who we are and what is at the core of our being.

If humanity is to survive we must recapture such values and natural instincts that reflect the human persons nobility and indeed real humanity. C.S. Lewis in his wonderful book, <u>Mere Christianity</u>, recounts the varying capacities of living organisms. For example there is no such thing as a really bad worm, or a really good one for that matter! But one could say that one has a good dog, or a bad one. But regarding a human person there can be incredibly noble humans and incredibly base ones. One need look no farther than many governments around the world. Positions of power it seems are merely, and sadly, primarily an opportunity for personal wealth and future security. I was told that a certain African leader made a statement in public remarks that education is only for the rich and powerful. The level of corruption in this African country is seemingly immense. At the expense of their own people the corrupt leaders seem to have little concern with providing the most basic infra-structure.

It is something that should anger any person who longs for justice. Such noble sentiments of anger fueled wrong headed attempts grouped as "Liberation Theology" which served ultimately to replace one oppressor for another. One need look no farther then the debacle in Haiti in which a priest actually gave up his own priesthood to become the president. In a matter of time the ex-priest seemingly did nothing more than oppress those who had been the oppressors. He even seemed to forget the poor that he set out to liberate. I was talking to another priest from Peru who noted that for all the efforts of the Liberation Theologians, their efforts to "liberate" left behind few schools, or hospitals, or real development to benefit the poor and the downtrodden.

To quote the recent *Batman Begins* movie, "it is not who we are, but what we do that defines us!" This captures a value that is deeply Christian. The Christian witness that contributed to bringing down the Roman Empire was the Church's care for the poor. The Christians cared for those who were on the margins of society, the weak, the poor the sick. They provided a social service by striving to care for the "unproductive" in society. They were the welfare system for the empire. They early Christians loved people because they were people. They recognized that they were serving Christ. They received no material benefit from their service. Christians must never become the oppressors of corrupt regimes, but must topple them by their persistent love and concern for the immortal soul of their oppressors. It may take generations, but we are talking about eternal realities, so what is the big deal. The Israelites toiled for hundreds of years under the oppression of the pharaohs, should not Christians be able to do the same? The Israelites did not lose faith, neither should we! Those who are blinded by evil will ultimately destroy themselves. Those who embrace the truth and all that is good will be exonerated and respected in the end.

The funeral of John Paul II testifies to the enormous respect that he commanded, and I would argue that the reason for that great tribute was the respect he had for others. His love for Christ was reflected in his ability to love others truly and sincerely. His funeral was believed to be the largest media event in world history to date! John Paul II was profoundly aware that freedom is part and parcel of human dignity. If there is no freedom there can be no love, and no real faith. No one can force a person to believe in any meaningful way. It can be credibly argued that the early Christians made this mistake when the Emperor converted to Christianity. It is easy to give into the pressure of belief, when the other option is death or prison. Faith can only be true when it is lived in freedom! I deeply appreciate the great freedom that this country affords her people. I truly believe its laws can serve to guide humanity to a brighter future. This future can be realized when people respect everyone, especially the most vulnerable.

It is important for humanity's future that people realize how important their role is in God's plan. Mysteriously, or as a miracle of grace, I some how got the idea that my choices really do make a difference in the world. My choices do not just affect me. Freedom comes with profound responsibility. I truly am profoundly indebted to my parents for the appreciation and value of others that they helped me to grasp. Even though my father died when I was only 16, he provided an excellent example of faith and commitment to Jesus, and in particular to His Most Sacred Heart. My mother died when she was 73 and truly was known as someone who would say nothing bad about anyone. They were a great example of married love.

My own personal experience drove me to the query, if unrequited human love causes such pain to the individual, what must God experience when His Divine love is rejected? I would argue that this is a fruitful reflection. In my younger days, a few years after the death of my father, I have to admit that I had an experience that was painful at the time, but which I feel tremendously deepened my own insight into human relationships. I cared deeply for a young woman, and that person did not share those same feelings for me. This experience, however, led me to reflect on a simple fact stated slightly differently above: if unrequited human love causes such pain, what must our Lord feel when he loves us with divine love and we fail to love Him? (Quite a big cut above human love) Sadly it seems so many of His people blow Him off! At this time in my life I was not seriously entertaining the idea of priesthood, but in my prayer at the time I asked that this particular woman may have a change of heart. If that was not in God's plan, I prayed that I might meet someone that God knew better than I and would better serve His purposes. I even prayed that if God wanted me to be a priest, I would do it. All I asked was that I might understand things more clearly.

In fact, some years later, I met a wonderful Catholic woman who had a deep faith, but I also felt that God may be calling me to the priesthood. So here I am! Honestly I cannot imagine myself being any happier doing anything else. I often borrow and modify a line from a popular radio talk show host, "the priesthood is more fun than a human being should be allowed to have". Good choices sometimes take great sacrifices, but they are worth it. Unlike evil choices, good choices are self-constructive - not self-destructive. It is never too late to love God. He is waiting for our response and will only rejoice in the gift of our devotion and love.

I still sometimes marvel at they way I came to my own personal decisions. It saddens me when I reflect on how many people make such poor choices in their life decisions. Often times these choices are conditioned by the dysfunctional families which are so rampant today. Love is glorious when it is mutual and freely given. Sadly it seems many confuse sexual attraction or the animalistic sex drive as the main motivation for choosing a partner. Such attitudes erode humanity's hope. If humanity is to survive as a whole, we need to recapture the great dignity of the family. A family is comprised of human beings with equal dignity; a family is indeed a community of persons. The world must come to recognize sex as a gift to be used to build up the human family and deepen one's ability to be truly a giver of life.

Love is at the heart of humanity's future. Love was also at the heart of my decision to be a priest. Love not only applies to relationships, but it must be ordered to all that is good, just and free. One can love their country or "state", but the "state" or government will never successfully force such a response from its subjects. If true hope is to be realized it can only be done so in the context of true freedom. Religion can not be forced any more than true love can be forced. If various religious traditions can ever become secure enough in themselves, there will be no need for any religious tradition to use coercion to further their cause. It is such coercion that has given the religious pursuit such a bad name. Truth is what must be the uniting force for the human family: real truth, historical truth, and indeed scientific truth. Truth must never be feared, but pursued. Truth is indeed the source of our joy. St. Paul says it quite clearly, and I certainly agree, "If Christ is not risen from the dead, we are the most wretched of men!" This is indeed true. If Christ is not the Son of God, than humans are really no different from the baby seals! Human dignity has no real singular value. But Jesus is the truth and I am convinced that history will vindicate my position. Humanity is wounded. We are blinded by what I call original sin. Sadly, it is not so easy to recognize the truth.

As I was riding the train to Cologne for World Youth Day in 2005, I had the great pleasure of meeting a man who was sharing his insights regarding the importance of Mary, the mother of Jesus, and her assumption into heaven. I was struck by his truly joyful demeanor. He had a theological degree and had written to Cardinal Ratzinger, now Benedict XVI, when he was in charge of the Congregation for the Doctrine of the Faith. Cardinal Ratzinger at that time praised his concepts and seemed genuinely interested in his work. What was so interesting was this individual was also a Mathematician. He was getting ready to publish a paper that would be instrumental, he believed, in addressing some of the mathematical problems one encounters in quantum mechanics. He also believed that the problem he solved could potentially contribute to the solution of the unified field theory that Einstein had worked on up to his death. He had worked on this problem for twenty years and believes that he has found a solution; a solution that, he believes, could be the greatest mathematical breakthrough in this millennium. His excitement and joy at his potential discovery was inspiring. The point to this discussion is that real truth always leads to joy. When we discover the truth, no matter what its form, scientific or theological, we will find and experience a deep and abiding joy.

There seems to be great cycles in societies and cultures. I can remember hearing somewhere a reflection on how humanity seems to be trapped in a cycle which, from the Jewish account, begins in freedom. Freedom then leads to complacency, from complacency to apathy, from apathy to oppression, from oppression to revolution, from revolution back to freedom. If societies fail to operate under the rule of law (that is presuming good and just laws of course), true development will be stifled. If governments do not truly exist to serve and protect the common good they are headed to their own demise. One needs look no farther than many third world governments where officials often live in comfort and opulent luxury while most of their people suffer. This fosters instability, resentment and hostility. This certainly feeds into this tragic cycle, a cycle which is hauntingly applicable to the great cultures of the world, from the Jewish Kingdom, to the Roman Empire, even to now in our own experience in the United States. The only way this cycle can be broken is by recognizing the human person's true dignity.

Hope always lies in truth and truth will ultimately win the day. As previously mentioned, evil always has a profound self-destructive tendency. There are many highly educated people, but unfortunately they have been formed with bad information or fallen prey to their own selfishness. If people truly would like to eradicate poverty and look out for the working man, then why would they embrace policies that destroy their own populations, such as abortion and contraception? I really do not embrace any political party, and quite frankly I think if anyone blindly embraces a party for the party's sake they are making a grave error.

Politics are important because people need to have structures to foster a stable and just society. I remember a conversation I had with one of my parishioners. This man had been in politics and in fact was the mayor of a rather large metropolitan area. He was clearly a Democrat. He pulled me aside at a church function and said,

"Father, do you know what the difference between a Democrat and a Republican is?" he paused and said, "They are spelled differently!" Sad to say but I think there is more truth than fiction in those words. Many politicians seem to take issues as the result of political calculation, as opposed to what is the truth or ultimately for the common good. One can find a quote from Ted Kennedy that was stanchly pro-life! Now the man seems to endorse every form of abortion which includes what is called a partial-birth abortion. This grisly and gruesome method entails inducing a dangerous breech birth (feet first so the head is in the birth canal) and then one plunges a sharp object at the base of a child's neck to kill the child before the head is delivered. This is wicked and evil and points to a deep and profound blindness and disrespect for life. There is certainly room for debate as to how heavy should a populous be taxed, but there is not middle ground on whether we should allow members of our community to kill other genetically complete human beings as the result of some goofy idea of privacy!

There have been some high profile cases in the media over the years; at the writing of this work, there has been a person recently sentenced to death for killing his pregnant wife, and a rock star who allegedly has abused children. There is a degree of common sense that still prevails on some level, but it has to be very confusing to these misguided souls. If a person can kill a child before it leaves the womb, the greatest form of abuse, then why not be able to see others as merely an object to be manipulated and used if done in the privacy of one's own home? I am amazed at how many people will attack others, but are so blind to their own faults. How many people are able to recognize that a child has not the ability to give consent in terms of abuse, but at the same time fail to recognize the great damage done as the result of sexual relations between consenting adults outside of marriage?

The real problem is that many abusers really do not believe that what they are doing is wrong. After all, many in our world want to believe that if you think it is ok, it is ok after all. I mean, someone needs to hear a tree fall in the words for it to make a sound, right? Obviously this is ridiculous to suggest a person determines what is true. Many in our world have embraced many ridiculous concepts in the past, from slavery, to now, abortion on demand. The failure to recognize human dignity is at the root of all these problems. Should we not be able to recapture common sense? It is sad, but it seems that those who fail to grasp common sense often endorse policies that kill their own constituencies. As I said before, evil will always destroy itself, so it is safe to say that they will lose power, hopefully, sooner than later.

Human Dignity demands respect, even for those people who fail to respect others. The truth will win, if all can come to embrace it. If those who suffer under oppressive regimes can love their oppressors and strive to be a force for good in society, the evil regimes will ultimately collapse upon themselves. It is not through revolution that corrupt regimes will be overcome but by love and adherence to all that is true. God will always remain faithful to those who are faithful to Him. Ultimately that means recognizing that God's creation is good and His creatures will be the solution to all problems and never the problem themselves.

I guess if I had a dream it would be of a united humanity that sees humans as an asset, not a liability. The world population growth would be addressed not as a problem, but a blessing. This gift would be the motivation to explore new solutions aimed at survival and care, not death and destruction. Maybe colonies under the ocean or in space are not so nearly far fetched as one might imagine. If military spending were not aimed at killing others, but truly protecting life and making places inhabitable, then we could truly start working together as a human family. If God did create other races in the stars, He might be relying on us to proclaim the Gospel to them!

There is hope for humanity, namely the hope that rests in discovering the truth as it is. Human beings do have value. We will be best served when we serve others and recognize their dignity.

Chapter XII ·
Why do they call me father?

What it really means to be called father.

As I write this reflection I am in my forties. I have been a priest since 1992 and it is only in this new millennium that I have been more deeply appreciating what it means to be a father. A good father has to say hard things to his children. A good father has to form his children and help his children know how valuable they are and how important it is for them to make good judgments.

There are many fathers who are not good ones. They are not involved in their children's lives and sometimes are actually contributing to the demise of their own offspring. My heart aches when I hear (and I have seen) the plight of some children whether in rural or city areas. Just recently a distraught parishioner related that her great grand niece was the daughter of what she described as a crack-whore. Child-Protective Services at the time had to locate the child. Sadly, the child is left to experience that hellish existence, at least for a time.

Good fathers are pained when they see their own children get themselves in painful situations, but good fathers will always be the first to show mercy and not say "I told you so", but rather "today is the beginning of the rest of your life!" Good fathers will say the hard things and patiently even discipline their own children, usually suffering themselves, more than the suffering inflicted on their children as a result of the discipline.

I recall a couple I was preparing for marriage. I related to them, in a very clear way, the teachings of Christ and His Church. The woman was a diabetic as I recall and pregnancy was a real danger. I certainly empathized with her, but nonetheless, clearly related that artificial contraception was not an option for a Catholic who wanted to live her faith. She was a chemist or a biologist and gifted intellectually. It wasn't until years later that I ran into her at an area church function. She shared with me that I had made her so angry as I was preparing them for marriage and that the church's teaching seemed to be just ridiculous at the time, presumably not unlike what many young children must think about their parent's rules. I knew she wasn't pleased with me at the time, but I always feel that I am not being fair to anyone if I don't tell them the truth to the best of my ability and understanding. She went on to relate how she came to see the wisdom of the Church and expressed her deep gratitude to me. It was because I was able to say the hard things that she started to question her own perspectives. Her respect for the Church had been profoundly deepened.

On the other hand, I can recall in the seminary a person relating the story of a "pastoral" priest giving council to a woman who was considering an abortion. The priest, thinking he was being compassionate or "pastoral" said, "I will support whatever decision you make." The poor woman chose poorly, killed her child and came back and was very angry at the priest. I would argue that she was right to be angry; for had the priest given here sound council she may have had the courage to make the correct choice and would have not chosen to kill her child. The sad reality is that just because the Church is adamantly opposed to abortion, people who have been duped into making that horribly disordered and evil choice feel the Church will not forgive them. This is the greatest error anyone can make. The greatest sin of Judas, Christ's betrayer, was not the betrayal, but the unwillingness to accept the forgiveness of Jesus. Peter denied Jesus three times, but he was humble enough to own his mistake and receive the forgiveness of the Lord..

One of the greatest gifts of being a priest is being able to lift the burdens of those who have been deceived and have done incredibly horrible things. They, for a time, had been blinded and thinking that there was no forgiveness for them. When they come to realize that it is all about mercy, and they are open to it, the joy and peace they experience is nothing short of miraculous.

I also know of a situation where a person formally left the church to be "ordained" by another minister who seemed to appoint himself as his own ultimate authority. The person who formally left the church did so after being diagnosed with a serious illness. Sadly, he also then was diagnosed with terminal cancer. I never for a moment questioned the sincerity of this man, and at the end of his life he was open to the sacraments and was willing to recognize that if he was mistaken, he certainly was sorry for whatever he did wrong. He made a profession of faith in the Church. Even though it seemed many around him judged the Church very harshly, he was open to the truth in the end.

The greatest danger for us all, which is epitomized in the lives of children, is to think that we do know everything, or assume that no one else can know anything. Then in turn, with that logic in place, we can do whatever we want. The world does not work this way, and any good father knows that he must never let his children make the rules when they are not equipped with the experience and knowledge to do so.

Many issues are difficult. Divorce and remarriage outside the Church is a challenging pastoral problem. Many seem to be openly defiant and are not open to the remedies the church offers.The real tragedy in our world is that most people do not think they are in need of mercy. Many do not think they do anything wrong. Many people who have found themselves in bad marriages have divorced and remarried. They do not hesitate to come to communion. In fact, they again are angry at the Church for following the prescriptions of the bible. St. Paul makes it clear that if a person takes communion while not realizing the full implications of such an act, that communion brings condemnation on the person, and not redemption or full communion with the mystical body of Christ. The Church's teaching is aimed at striving for true unity and not seeing the Eucharist as a very nice symbol that makes us feel warm inside when we receive it.

The confusion is rampant on this issue. As I stated previously my custom at weddings and funerals is to say something like, "We believe as Catholics that this is truly the Body and Blood of Christ, and when we take it, we are saying that we believe in everything that the Catholic Church teaches and professes to be true. For that reason the Church feels she has no right to impose that obligation of belief on those who are not Catholic, or those Catholics who have not been practicing their faith." These clear instructions often bring dialogue, and often times the dialogue is incredibly fruitful.

As a priest, one is in the extremely privileged position to guide souls along a path which helps them to value themselves above things. Let us recall again that little pithy phrase which seems so apropos here: *God made us to love people and use things, sadly most people love things and use people.* A good father is able to help people realize how important it is not to use other people. A good father will help others use the gifts they have to make our world a better place.

I think I can actually imagine the joy of parents when they finally see their children respecting each other and not fighting and bickering all the time. I really have come to appreciate more deeply what it means to be a father. My role as priest is a spiritual father, but our spiritual lives are enmeshed in the physical realities of life. Physical maturity and spiritual maturity are two different things. A good father is one who helps his children gracefully mature on every level!

Chapter XIII · What is the Meaning of Life, and how to be a Real Survivor?

It was Bishop Fulton Sheen who related that all people are drawn to life, love and truth. It is in these things one finds true meaning in life. When we truly allow ourselves to value life, pursue real love and seek ultimate truth, we are indeed on the path that will lead to our eternal survival. Humanity's future is bright only if it can be open enough and free enough to embrace the fullness of reality. I would go so far as to say to pursue such things is truly humanity's only hope. The human person is tremendously resilient, but our technology today is making it very easy for the human person to be the instrument of humanity's own destruction. Humans are too often seen as objects to be used and manipulated rather than *subjects* to be loved and valued!

The Politically Correct

I am often amazed at people who want to be associated with the Catholic faith, and then do their best to reflect the antithesis of what it means to be truly Catholic. A political candidate was quick to reveal that he was a Catholic, and a question was posed to him, "Who were your heroes?" He suggested that his heros were Christopher Reeves and Michael J. Fox, both of whom had suffered debilitating health conditions. I found it odd that those individuals would have been his choice, but certainly political correctness is epitomized by such choices. Michael J. Fox, afflicted with Parkinson's disease, and Christopher Reeves, who suffered from a debilitating fall from a horse, were seen to be champions of embryonic stem cell research. It seems odd that a catholic would not mention John Paul II, who also struggled with Parkinson's, but would never have thought of sacrificing the life of another human for his own benefit.

Why are people so reticent to explain the huge difference in the benefits between embryonic stem cell research and adult stem cell research? To date I am not aware of one usable therapy that has come from embryonic stem cell research, and nearly one hundred usable therapies have been developed from the use of adult stem cells.[126] Embryonic stem cell research has used techniques approved by Hitler's Mengala, using humans as nothing more than laboratory specimens, while adult stem cell research does not kill developing humans for its incredible gains. Society is doomed, in worldly terms, if we lose the sense of human life and its dignity. If we fail to recognize the value of human life as absolute then the movie I Robot, and the popular series, Battlestar Galactica, where machines become our chief adversaries, may reflect and predict an ominous future that is not so inconceivable.

What does it mean to be a Catholic? St. Augustine said in the early centuries of Christianity something like, "many people consider themselves Catholic, but are Catholic only in name. Others do not consider themselves Catholic, but indeed are Catholic as evidenced in their lives." I think this great witness to Christ and His Church is recognized in the lives of many non-Catholic Christians and other people of good will of all other faith traditions. John Paul II recognized a prominent agnostic for his pro-life views. He acknowledged that this man, who claimed no explicit faith, was still a champion for truth. We will be saved by truth; Catholics believe the fullness of truth is simply Jesus Christ. All salvation is through Christ alone. The Church does not exclude from salvation those who

---

126 One needs to look no further than the National Catholic Bioethics Quarterly Journal, 6399 Drexel Road, Philadelphia, PA 19151-2511. Web site: www.ncbcenter.org

claim no explicit knowledge of Christ. A prominent theologian, Karl Rahner, called such enlightened souls, anonymous Christians, but salvation can only come through Christ!

To be Catholic is to recognize the fundamental implications of the Incarnation. What does that loaded theological term mean? Incarnation means nothing less then recognizing the person of Christ in every human being on earth, both conceived and yet to be conceived. This is why the Catholic Church is viewed as being so "hung up" on life. This view is truly the key to humanity's survival.

A person asked me about a woman who he thought was Catholic. The school was considering inviting her to speak at an assembly for all the students. I was not familiar with the name, but I felt it was important to do a little research about her. As it turned out, she did claim to be Catholic, in fact a Catholic author, and a Catholic religious sister. I read a few articles that this person wrote and I found myself saddened at her lack of insight. She seemed to be more politically correct than theologically so. She seemed quick to point out the problems with the recent War on Terror, but concluded that the only reason why the Church is opposed to abortion and artificial contraception was because, as she charged, the Church was hung up on sex. I am no psychologist, but I suspect there is a little projection going on there!

Clearly there is sin in the world, and sin deforms the body of Christ in gross ways. The graphic portrayal of Christ's suffering in Mel Gibson's' portrayal of the passion shows the ugliness in the human person's brutality. Can you see God in the brutalized image of Christ? As Christians we believe that God became man for us. Jesus prays, "Father, may they be one in me, as I am one in you". Jesus is no metaphor for divinity. Jesus is divinity itself in the flesh. I marvel at how so few people seem to grasp the simple value that the Church places on human life. History is a cruel teacher, but so many people seem to be such poor students! Nonetheless I refuse to lose hope.

There was a time not so very long ago in the United States that a man was judged merely by the color of his skin. The institution of slavery was finally conquered by right thinking. I think it would be safe to say that most would be horrified to introduce legislation that would re-institute slavery as a legitimate institution. But yet there has become a whole class of people who have lost their right to be free, only this time it is not the result of race or creed, but age. Humans in the early stages of development have no right to life.

I was once in an airport with a person who seemed to be a legitimate and first rate scholar. The person seemed to be an expert in the ancient biblical languages and yet seemed unable to grasp how logically a person can accept no other point than conception or the joining of the gamete cells, the ova and the sperm, as the point of origin for a genetically complete human being. This person seemed to suggest that there may be some arbitrary point when this process somehow becomes a developing human. Maybe the moon is made out of green cheese, too! The DNA defines every characteristic of the human, down to the number of hair follicles on one's head. Pope Benedict XVI recently noted that the person is more than their DNA, and that is true; but even for the person who is not religious, it seems obvious that DNA certainly is integral to understanding the singular and peculiar nature of the human person. Age makes no difference in the value of that life. Both mother and child are of equal worth.

Not to beat the same old dead horse, but truth can never be determined or defined by the human person. Under the normal course of things, a pen falls to the ground when dropped, and people die when they are blown up. Embryonic stem cell research is as ridiculous as using children in orphanages for organ donors. Would any reasonable person suggest, "after all, nobody wants them, why not just cut them to pieces and farm out their parts for those children who are loved and wanted by parents who can afford the medical treatment?" Hopefully we have not become so calloused as to be less than horrified by such a proposal. Yet people will irrationally respond, "That is different". How is it different? Under the proper conditions, that orphan will develop into a full grown human person; likewise the embryo too, before it is conditioned to be an embryonic stem cell, will mature as an adult human. The Church serves to be the conscience of the world. It will be relentless in helping the human person realize his or her true value, even when individuals fail to recognize their own dignity.

The Church is an amazing organization that transcends essentially all cultures. This was clearly evident by the gathering of priests on the Island of Malta in 2004. The group was comprised of nearly 1000 priests from 83 countries and over 200 dioceses from around the world. The amazing thing is that even though there were different cultures and different languages, there was a commonality that transcended all these natural barriers. I found this epitomized on the ferry as we traveled from Malta to Gozo. On deck there was a conversation between an Iraqi priest, a priest from Israel, and priests from France and the United states. We could talk and be as brothers united for a single cause, Jesus Christ, the redeemer and savior of the entire world. He is the only hope for our world: I have come to believe this, and the event that transpired on the deck of that ferry provides the greatest evidence that such a hope seems to be well founded. It truly seems to me worth spending one's life on working towards that goal of human solidarity. If one truly embraces that goal, they will have a deep and profound respect for the religious liberty of others. For if a person knows Jesus, they will be able to recognize him in the face of those who follow Mohammad, Buddha, and the Hindu faith, as well as all other religions of the world. All things are not equal. I can not prove that I am correct, anymore than I can prove that Jesus rose from the dead, but there were witnesses and I have come to believe them.

Faith in Christ will lead to a deep and profound love for each and every human being, whether it be Catholics who have lost their way, or those who have been trapped by hideous addictions and sin. Only through love can we ever truly hope to conquer such enemies. Through integrity and common sense we will make progress.

If the world fails to recognize the truth about the human person, which I believe to be the infinite worth of every human being, it will continue down the path of terror, hatred and division. But if the world can come to its senses and merely recognize that things are knowable, things can be understood, maybe not perfectly, but more and more completely, then and only then can we begin to make headway towards real solutions. If the culture war is lost and the world chooses to believe that things are merely the way humans perceive them to be, then there can be no hope for real progress or understanding among peoples. If truth wins the day, then there can be peace, a peace that is much more than merely a cessation of hostility, but rather tranquil love that is motivated by a deep appreciation of every human being. The Culture of Life will indeed overcome the Culture of Death.

Times it seems I made a difference

Even when I was a seminarian I felt as though there were times when I had the opportunity to make a real positive impact on someone's life. I recall one day a rather frazzled looking man came to the door. I think I was alone in the rectory, so the resident priest was not there. He still wanted to talk to me.

He related a story, that as I recall consisted of a tragic situation.. He had a successful company that he and a friend had been operating. I believe that there had been a million dollars in sales the last year the company had functioned in the late eighties. It seems to me that his friend had gone through a divorce and lost half the company's assets as a result of the settlement. Then he, in turn, had suffered the same horrible plight, divorce. I believe divorce is worse than death: the betrayal, the failure, and that nagging underlying thought, "what could I have done to not cause this?" As the result of this tragedy, the company was now totally defunct, all assets were frozen and he had no car and was riding a bicycle to and from his work, which was to my recollection, a basic janitorial service job.

The situation was ugly. He had no car, there was a restraining order against him, even most of his clothes were locked into a house in which he now had no access. He was riding a bicycle and saw a man in "his" car, wearing "his" clothes, and presumably living in his old house with his old wife. He went ballistic and needed to talk to someone and that someone was me. I listened mostly. The man was not Catholic, by the way, but the church in which I was a summer seminarian must have been the first church he found. I certainly empathized with him. I may have related the deep betrayal that our Lord must have experienced, and quite frankly I do not remember what exactly I said. I didn't think it was particularly edifying, but when he left I remember him thanking me. What really blew me away was that he suggested that I had just prevented him from committing murder. We must never underestimate the impact we can have on a person's life by simply taking the time to listen.

The priest's task is primarily to present the Gospel, which entails both the cross and resurrection, as the way to salvation. The cross is the way we can overcome all obstacles. By understanding the mystery of the cross we can then present, in a convincing way, the challenge of the Christian way of life. It is through the cross that we hope in our resurrection. I seem to recall that some scholars reported that where Paul preached using philosophy and logic, like in the *Areopagus* in Athens, the Gospel did not rapidly take root. When Paul preached that the Gospel was scandal to the Jews and absurdity to the Greeks, people could relate to the real power of the cross and the message. It is interesting to note that the Gospel seemed to more rapidly flourish in these areas by some historical accounts.

Philosophy and scholarship are important, but when the philosopher's child dies or one's spouse becomes terminally ill, all the logic in the world cannot overcome the realities of personal suffering. Hope that is found in the Gospel of Christ enables one to confront these realities in a meaningful and constructive way.

When we understand the cross we begin to understand all the various teachings of the Church, whether it be Natural Family Planning or the subtleties of the teachings on Capitol Punishment. Catholics then see the value of Natural Family Planning and how a real priority is placed on life and not mutual gratification. Sinful choices can often lead to bigger problems, such as an unwanted pregnancy, or even devastating diseases such as AIDS or a host of other venereal diseases. I do not know what led to that man's divorce or where the principle blame rested, but the fact remains that sin leads to bad things, and bigger sins lead to bigger bad things.

Chapter XIV · Who do you say that I am?

This is the question that every sincere Christian must confront in his or her life. It is the question that Jesus posed to the early leaders of the Church. The way we answer this question will impact every dimension of our life. I recall John Paul II's opening line of his first encyclical, "The Redeemer of Man, Jesus Christ is the center of the universe and history." Many people do not believe this statement, but I have chosen to accept it through faith. I only wish that I could more fully live what I profess. It is easy to get caught up in theological platitudes or pithy definitions such as "The God of infinite distance becomes infinitely close to us in Christ."[127] The important aspect of this faith is how it is translated into our response to God and to each other.

In the book, Remembering Jesus Christ, [128] Cantalamessa invites us to focus on the message of the early Christians. The message was simple, Christ is risen, truly He is risen! While Jesus left quite a wake in His path, e.g. the Church, we must never lose sight of the Church's source, Christ Himself. I personally do not generally hear voices or

---

127 Karl Rahner, a prominent theologian in the 20th century.

128 Raniero Cantalamessa, Remember Jesus Christ: Responding to the Challenges of Faith in Our Time (Paperback) by (Author), Marsha Daigle_ Williamson (Translator), Word Among Us Publisher, 2007.

have some monopoly on what God intends, but it seems to me there can be some clear indications of who this Jesus is.

One can reflect on the deeply speculative nature of Jesus' identity, but I am not too convinced that would be all that helpful. We don't really need to know the inner workings of a power plant to be able to effectively use a light switch. It is nice to know that stuff, as it is nice to know the wonderful distinctions that the scholastic theologians have given us, but for many it may not be that helpful. What is it about Jesus that can invite people to live their lives in total service to God and to others? A good friend of mine invited me to reflect on this, and so here is my meager attempt to reflect on who I say Jesus is!

Jesus is Lord, consubstantial with the Father, light from light, true God from true God, begotten, and not made, it is through Him all things are made for us and for our salvation, which is ultimately being one with God. He did indeed come from heaven and suffered, was crucified, died and was buried, and on the third day rose from the dead. He will indeed return to judge the living and the dead and this kingdom will have no end and that new Kingdom will exceed even the life of the universe as we know it. This pretty much covers the doctrinal stuff, but there is more.

Somehow, somewhere there comes a time when we are introduced to the Gospel, the Good News. Many people are informed of Jesus as the central figure in their faith, or merely a historical figure that lived long ago. As for me, Jesus was and is the person who suffered for us. Call it what you might but I was conditioned to see Jesus as God and as a reality that invited our attention. Jesus is a person who is always concerned about our best interest. God's will was something that was good for us, but not always easy to know or certainly do. I think to discern God's will, Christ's will, is to find the path to happiness and contentment. There is God's perfect will, and also God's general will. His general will is easy to know, avoid sin and do good! His perfect will can be a little more challenging to uncover. Children are blessed in that they are quick to believe without a full understanding of belief's ramifications. I hate to use the word gullible, but if someone happens to present that which it true to one who is gullible, then the gullible is blessed indeed for he or she has accepted the truth!

I believe Jesus is simply who He claims to be in the scriptural accounts, both Son of Man and Son of God. Jesus outrageously describes Himself as I AM! One of my favorite quotes says much,

> *If I do not perform my Father's works, do not believe me;*
> *but if I perform them, even if you do not believe me, believe*
> *the works, so that you may realize (and understand) that*
> *the Father is in me and I am in the Father."* [129]

It seems to be in vogue to call into question the veracity of the simple meaning of the bible. Many Scholars seem to suggest that such passages above are merely the result of the author's agenda and can not plausibly be attributed to something that Christ actually said. It is certainly not an easy task to interpret the fuller sense of such passages, but if the bible is just reduced to a form of rhetorical speech, (something that is concocted merely to persuade and has no allegiance to truth) it loses its force. I think most scholars often respond harshly to those Christians who seem to believe that the Bible fell out of the sky intact. But in reality, the Bible is the book written by a community of faith, for a community of faith, whose contents ultimately were discerned by a community of faith. Chaos results when people fail to believe in the power of the Holy Spirit to guide and form a community whose ultimate goal is unity; unity with Christ and unity with one another.

I believe that Jesus' ultimate mission was to simply glorify the Father, and this was to be accomplished by drawing the human race to the Father through Himself by the means and the agency of the Holy Spirit. Jesus invites us to be one with Him as He is one with the Father.

> *Consecrate them in the truth. Your word is truth. As*
> *you sent me into the world, so I sent them into the world.*
> *And I consecrate myself for them, so that they also may be*
> *consecrated in truth. "I pray not only for them, but also for*
> *those who will believe in me through their word, so that they*
> *may all be one, as you, Father, are in me and I in you, that*

---

129 John 10: 37-38

*they also may be in us, that the world may believe that you
sent me. And I have given them the glory you gave me, so
that they may be one, as we are one, I in them and you in
me, that they may be brought to perfection as one, that the
world may know that you sent me, and that you loved them
even as you loved me. Father, they are your gift to me. I
wish that where I am they also may be with me, that they
may see my glory that you gave me, because you loved me
before the foundation of the world. Righteous Father, the
world also does not know you, but I know you, and they
know that you sent me. I made known to them your name
and I will make it known, that the love with which you
loved me may be in them and I in them."* [130]

I think it can be argued that humanity's only hope lies in an
understanding of radical solidarity. Throughout human history those
who are in control seem to do what they can to entrench their own
superiority. Jesus who is in ultimate control reveals His ability to
turn the world on its head. He invites everyone to recognize their
own dignity and shows mercy to those who certainly do not deserve
it. Unlike social structures that claim a certain superiority over
another, Jesus takes on the role of servant. Can you really imagine
what a government would be like if its administrators were truly and
principally concerned with the welfare of the people and not merely
holding on to their own power? Communism makes the state god,
while Capitalism makes personal wealth god. Jesus wants us to see
the mechanisms of this world to serve unity and goodness. Both
the government and profit are to serve people and not the other way
around.

Problems in the world are huge, Jesus knew that, but He also
knew that this world is only a means to the Father. As individuals
we can do little to solve the corruption and sin in the structures of
the world, but we can impact those that we touch. Jesus knew this
and sent the apostles on a mission that would change the world one
soul at a time.

---

130 New American Bible, John 17: 17-26

I can remember hearing the Roman Canon when I was in high school and the phrase, "You know how firmly we believe in you and dedicate ourselves to you" and that phrase was a little scary. In reality I could say I do believe but how firmly? I could still see myself not being as kind as I should be, or as generous as I should be, or as loving as I should be; and dedicated? I really felt as though I was not all that dedicated to God, I followed pretty much my own pursuits, sure I was avoiding the big sins it seemed, I was not taking advantage of women, or getting drunk, or abusing drugs, but I didn't seem to be doing all that much that revealed real dedication. Avoiding sin, is just not being stupid. Sin harms us and others, so avoiding sin is just good for us. God gets nothing out of us avoiding sin, other than the fact that He is spared of seeing His creation destroy itself.

I think Jesus looks at this world and weeps through His people who thirst for justice. The idea of the Incarnation is way more than just Jesus coming for a visit around 0 BC to 33AD. Jesus invites us to be in real solidarity with Him. He knows what it is to suffer because He became more than a passive observer. Jesus became one with us. He is the one who reveals to us the fullness of our potential as human beings. He was not a human person in the strict theological sense of the term, but He was indeed fully human. His oneness with us reveals the infinite capacity of human nature.

It is easy to despair of the human condition. Many governments are rife with corruption and greed, and thus contribute to a flagrant disrespect for life and human dignity in our world. Much of foreign aid seems only to help those in power and little finds its way to alleviate the true suffering that many endure. Pope Benedict called on the United Nations to follow its founding principles. The United Nations has had its own problems with corruption. Jesus just invites us to minimize human suffering by recognizing the dignity of each and every person and their infinite potential. He invites us to find peace and happiness, not by seeking the praise of others, but by doing what we can to serve others. We are called to help others recognize their dignity and their worth as humans, simply because they are human!

I think Mother Theresa was a person who knew Jesus, she saw Him in every person she served. She did not let the hopelessness that pervaded her, overcome her. She truly seemed to get it! "Whatsoever you do to the least of my people, that you do unto me!" (Mt. 25:40) The world's problem is that it has nothing to believe in, many have succumbed to the belief that we are truly alone, and we must really look out for only oneself. Hatred can only be conquered by love. Jesus is love! God is love, Love is one! When the person experiences love, he is willing to make heroic sacrifices for the beloved. Jesus loved and loves us and demonstrated that love by His suffering and death. Can the world imitate this love? Can leaders really take their responsibility seriously and have a true and genuine concern for those who are subject to their authority? Those who know Christ can be content to some extent with being victimized, but they will be more concerned with how the victimizer is imperiling their own soul. Jesus' own words on the cross point to this when He cries out, "Forgive them Father, for they know not what they are doing!" It is hard to see so clearly, it is impossible for the human person to love so purely; but with God, all things are possible.

So, "Who do you say that I am?" For me the answer lies in the face of every human person, Jesus, in addition to His full and perfect abiding presence with the Father and the Holy Spirit in the beatific vision of heaven is found in every human being from the moment of their conception to their dying breath; from that point those who have accepted the invitation to love and be open to the truth will find themselves destined to be one with the Father, as Jesus is one with Him.

Conclusion

So let me try and summarize my thoughts and attempt to directly answer the question, "Why am I a priest?" I have always had a passion for the truth. And through the grace of God I have come to believe in Jesus Christ, the God-Man who inaugurated his Church, knowing full well that there would be traitors among the ranks. Sadly, Judas had probably convinced himself that he was doing the right thing, not unlike many dissidents today. He may have thought that his way was better and more politically effective. Only through prayer and our perfection in charity can we hope to gain real insight into the truth as it actually is. I truly believe traitors are those who fail to defend life, who have been so self-deceived that they can go through ritual actions, such as praying the rosary or celebrating the most perfect prayer, the Holy Sacrifice of the Mass, and yet fail to recognize the great dignity of the human person, the human person in their original innocence of their natural beginning. As the account handed to us goes, even Jesus chose twelve apostles and one was a traitor, hopefully 8.33% or 1/12 of the bishops are not traitors today. But can the Church hope to have a better track record than the Son of God Himself?

Ultimately it is quite simple. I have come to believe in Jesus and His Church like I have come to believe in Australia! I have come to trust the word of those who have seen Him. I have seen Christ with the eyes of faith. Every time I take the Sacred Host in my hands or gaze at Him during periods of adoration, I believe He is there, and sometimes the prayer of the man in the Gospel is my own, "Lord I believe, help my unbelief". I believe this because I simply have come to trust the testimony of others. People have seen Australia, I have even supposedly met people from Australia, but I have never seen it with my own eyes. True, I can get on a plane and go there, but I believe that when I will die, I will also go to Jesus' place.

As a priest, I do not have all the answers, but I do have many answers that give at least some meaning to life. John Paul II stated in his document on *The Christian Meaning of Human Suffering*, that there is always a dimension of incomprehensibility to human suffering, but with Christ our suffering can ultimately be the source of our joy. Any football player or great athlete or musician knows that sacrifices are made to attain mastery of some art. The pianist whose forearms burn with pain after hours of practice, or the athlete that pushes him or herself to the limits of one's physical capacity so that they are prepared for the competition, they know suffering. This suffering is only to gain a human skill. When we embrace the cross, when we choose not to give up, when we endure the hardships of life, our sacrifices will not go without reward. The reward is nothing less than perfect happiness.

Once I came to believe that Jesus is the way, the truth and the life, I felt I needed to follow the invitation I sensed. It certainly was a leap of faith, and if we are honest with ourselves our big choices always entail such a leap. My hope is that I may remain faithful and a witness to Christ. I have always had a passion for the truth, and I believe I have given myself the opportunity to serve the Truth, which is Love itself. I invite you to do the same, may you know your Master's Joy!

EPILOGUE

In this work I have spent a good deal of time reflecting on the thoughts of John Paul II. I felt as though I would be remiss if I did not reflect somewhat on the early works of Pope Benedict. I think it will serve to complete my reflections in a way that points us forward. The papacy has already been marked with controversy, whether it be his alleged insensitivity to the Moslem faith or even more recently towards the other Christian communities who are currently not in full communion with the Roman Catholic Church. I would argue that Benedict has been taken out of context and misunderstood. It is so sad that people seem so much more apt to look at things in the most negative way, as opposed to realizing that for real communication to actually transpire we need to actually listen to each other. Too often we can hear someone sarcastically say with a wave of the hand, "I hear you", rather than a focused and thoughtful response of, "I listened to you!" It is very important, even crucial, that we learn to listen to each other more attentively!

God is Love

Ultimately I am a priest and very happy as one because simply God is Love. This was the topic of Pope Benedict's first encyclical. True happiness can only be known in the experience of love. Every human being can understand this deep reality. To understand God most fully one must understand that God is indeed a God of Love. All legitimate religions attempt to grapple with this reality and serve to come to grips

183

with it. On the human level most people know this most intimately with their spouse and their personal relationships with family and friends.

In reading the encyclical I found myself experiencing real joy in the insights that seem so clearly related in Benedict's work. The pope reflects on how the church has often been mis-characterized as being hostile to human love. Pope Benedict is continuing to reflect and develop John Paul II's thoughts on love and its implications for humanity.

St. Augustine is often mischaracterized as not recognizing the beauty of human love. I would argue that this is a misreading. Augustine points out that when sexual relations are merely sought out to meet one's personal desire, such relations are a misuse of the sexual faculties. This is what I believe he meant when he says that if a man only has sex to relieve his sexual urge, even with his wife, he sins at least venially. I cannot imagine any woman being thrilled with the idea of having relations with her husband just to satisfy his biological drive. From the Christian perspective, this biological urge should serve to invite the person to express love. For the person who is pure of heart, he or she has the capacity to channel the desires in a way that is always marked by charity and self donation. Sex should never be merely reduced to an animalistic drive to satisfy oneself. Humans are different than the beasts because of our capacity to think and feel.

There is a beautiful quote from the pope's document and I use it in my presentation I give to married couples on the Pre-Cana preparation course we offer in our diocese. It follows:

> *That love between man and woman which is neither planned nor willed, but somehow imposes itself upon human beings, was called , ερος by the ancient Greeks. Let us note straight away that the Greek Old Testament uses the word , ερος only twice, while the New Testament does not use it at all: of the three Greek words for love, ερος, φιλιος (the love of friendship) and αγαπη, New Testament writers prefer the last, which occurs rather infrequently in Greek usage. As for the term φιλιος, the love of friendship, it is used with added depth of meaning in Saint John's Gospel in order to express the relationship between Jesus and his disciples* [131]

---

131 *Deus Caritas Est, n. 3.*

The pope acknowledges how important human love is. The world would have you believe that the church somehow rejects such love, but that is not the case. On the contrary the Church wants the human family to order its love in such a way that love is not somehow debased or merely reduced to an animalistic drive.

Charity, the Latin word for love, is something that is much more then giving things away. In fact sometimes people will give things away just so that they may then in turn exert control on the human person. Sad to say much of our world seems to distribute aid to the poor often with such conditions, or even worse the aid is merely used by criminals in the receiving country and misused to corrupt and control the masses. I have a friend from Nigeria who is actually angered when the US gives aid to his country because of its corruption. Most of the aid never finds its way to those who truly need it, but rather is consumed and lost in the corrupt bureaucracy. The world will be better served if we truly can strive to personally give things to the poor and not rely on institutions that have less than pure motives to be charitable.

Charity is more than just giving things away. For charity to be real it must be given in the appropriate spirit. Some people use material support as a means of manipulation as opposed to helping people out of a clear understanding of their dignity and their intrinsic worth.

Pope Benedict, some would suggest, is deeply influenced by St. Augustine. This case could be furthered on the pope's emphasis on the gratuitous nature of God's love. Augustine seems to suggest as a general theme throughout his works that God loves and loves freely. God's love is gratuitous in the positive sense of that term. God's love is meant to inspire a response and never to coerce it. If we truly understand what Jesus Christ did for us, we will be inspired to serve God. For Augustine, such an attitude is marked by those who dwell in the City of God. This is in direct contradiction with most people's experience with many individuals. Unlike God, many in our world not only seek praise for themselves, but strive to dominate through coercive force or other forms that are even more insidious. This attitude is exemplified in Augustine's understanding of the City of Man. Pope Benedict notes how sometimes even acts of Charity are used as tools of manipulation. Some people use foreign aid as a bargaining chip or a tool of manipulation. This is not how God operates!

Hopefully you have been fortunate enough to experience an act of gratuitous kindness. There are even some bright spots in the media. There was that powerful movie, *Pay it Forward*, which shows how the world can be radically changed by doing something for another. I have even noticed some commercials that highlight aspects of such acts expecting nothing in return. One entailed a couple of guys driving along on the highway and they notice a drink truck with an open side door, instead of taking some drinks for themselves, they made a risky move to close the door and prevent a potential accident. Also there was another ad which related people looking out for each other, holding a door open or avoiding some other mishap, ultimately the act is passed forward and goes full circle. The person who made the first kind act is a recipient of the kindness of another in the sequence of events he started. Sad to say most commercials seem to be more concerned about being selfish and thinking only of oneself. In other words, charity is totally lacking! The sensitive soul is indeed edified by such wonderful deeds of loving kindness. Ask yourself when you performed such a deed?

The Regensburg Affair

Pope Benedict in his Regensburg Lecture also made an attempt at deepening our mutual understanding. Sad to say and once again the pope was quick to be quoted out of context. The media chose to emphasize the polemical aspects of the debate, instead of focusing on the comments that led into what came to be the controversial remarks. The pope quotes the Koran where it reveres and promotes religious liberty:

> *In the seventh conversation (*4V8,.4. - controversy) edited by Professor Khoury, the emperor touches on the theme of the holy war. The emperor must have known that Surah 2, 256 reads: "There is no compulsion in religion".*[132]

Sadly the opportunity was lost to challenge our world to legitimate religious liberty and controversy instead ensued. The pope was not

---

132 Meeting with the Representatives of Science, Lecture of the Holy Father, Aula Magna of the University of Regensburg, Tuesday, 12 September 2006

swayed by the skeptics and courageously went to Turkey after the controversy. I have a friend who is from Turkey and was present during this papal visit. What I am about to relate may upset some conservative Christians, and his actions could also be misconstrued, but my friend reported how Pope Benedict not only "tolerated" the Muslim faith, but showed deep respect by actually bowing towards Mecca upon his arrival. I do not believe this was motivated by some shallow political savvy or some moral cowardice, but rather a deep and profound respect that recognizes the presence of Christ working in the souls of all who sincerely are seeking the truth.

Other Christian Communities

Pope Benedict has been striving to foster dialogue and he has done this by stating clearly the teachings of the Church. We must talk with one another if we ever hope to come to a deeper understanding of each other. As odd as it may sound, in the summer of 2007 I went on a fifteen hundred mile motorcycle trip with eleven evangelicals. It was quite the experience. Just a few weeks after the trip pope Benedict was restating the Church's position that the truth subsists in the Catholic Church and that all salvation is through the Church. I have come to expect the media to report things is such a way that really makes it difficult for the regular person to understand such things with any clarity. Needless to say, many people draw rash conclusions. I got an email soon after the media reports from one of the evangelicals who made the motorcycle trip with me, it went something like this, "So the pope says that I am going to hell!" I am so glad that he initiated the dialogue, remember, that was the pope's goal, and I was able to point him to the Second Vatican Council documents which clearly expresses what the Church is saying. It notes that all people who follow the truth and are concerned with truth can not necessarily be excluded from salvation. First place among the Body of Christ would be other Christian communities, a term that John Paul II felt to be a more nuanced and a less offensive way to express the council's "separated brethren" term. These other Christian communities revere the bible as the word of God and are most closely united to the Church. The Jews are recognized as the Chosen People of God, Jesus was a Jew, and how they indeed have the truth as God had revealed it to that point in history. Also we must see the followers of Mohammad as those who revere the Jewish Scriptures and even the Christian scriptures to some extent as well. The Koran recognizes practicing Jews and practicing Christians as people of the book.

The conciliar document, *Lumen Gentium*, continues by saying that all those who seek the truth, even if they have no explicit knowledge of God, are not to be necessarily excluded from salvation.[133] There seems to be room for even the magnanimous agnostic to be saved if he or she is striving to live a life concerned with goodness and truth! If they are seeking the truth, they indeed are seeking Jesus Christ.

The Pope and Jesus of Nazareth

The pope in his book on Jesus presents "his attempt to reveal the face of Jesus". He does so by clearly attempting to read the Scriptures with the eyes of faith. Faith helps one to see the bible as more than just a document that some people decided to write to push some kind of new world view. On the contrary the bible is a book written by a community of faith for a community of faith. There is a tendency to read the bible in isolation of a faith community. Much of modern scholarship, as helpful as it can be, often fails as a result of its own limitations. It often devolves into speculation over things that cannot be ascertained with any degree of reasonable certainty. Truth is a beautiful thing, and it will never lead anyone away from God and the ultimate reality of God, but when some present a "truth" that is not true, tremendous harm is done. The pope reflects on a method to read the scriptures while implementing such a method in his own reflections on Jesus and the implication of His claims.

I found one of the most interesting aspects of the book is his account of the dialogue with the Rabbi, Jacob Neusner, who wrote the book, A Rabbi Talks with Jesus. The candid discussion, specifically on aspects of the Gospel of Matthew, and the rabbi's willingness to intellectually engage the other, speaks of his broadness of mind and sincere desire to understand. Rabbi Neusner sets the stage by pointing to the longstanding tradition that argument reflects respect. If one respects the other person, even if they disagree with them, one will engage in a debate and challenge

133 Documents of Vatican II, *Lumen Gentium*, nn. 13-16, accessible from the Vatican Web site, www.vatican.va

the other person's perspectives. This is just what the Rabbi does and he confronts the radical claims that Jesus makes. Make no mistakes, Jesus does make radical claims. Jesus claims not only that He is the Messiah, but that He is God in the Flesh. Jesus has a mother because He is both God and Man, He entered the world through a woman. God had a mother! Jesus makes claims that only God could make. Jesus transcends the claims of the Torah, because in one sense Jesus is the Torah or the Word. Jesus claims that He can forgive sins, He claims to be Lord of the Sabbath. These claims can be interpreted to contradict the teaching that God had revealed to the Jews.

The book highlights the importance of engaging in dialogue and is willing to present things in such a way that real conversation can take place. There seems to be this cardinal secular virtue of tolerance. But this is a very bad thing. Would people who hope to truly forge a bond of mutual respect, only hope to tolerate the other? This is certainly not the case! Religious liberty is essential, religious tolerance is ultimately a destructive force.

The good news is that when Jesus returns the three great world religions will discover the aspects of the truth that they share. The Jews await the messiah, Christians await Jesus' return, while the Muslims believe that Jesus will return and vindicate their position. My hope is that we all can patiently wait for the resolution to this dilemma. If we can foster a deep and profound respect for one another, we can move beyond tolerance and deepen our respect for one another and truly promote true religious liberty.

Pope Benedict seems to be striving to do exactly this. He is willing to say the hard things, so that we might be drawn together to discuss such things and work towards real and lasting peace. This peace is far more than merely a cessation of hostility, but a peace that is rooted in deep and profound respect for the human person down to every last genetically complete human being!

In *Spe Salvi*, Pope Benedict's encyclical on *Saving Hope*, he points to the world's only hope, and that is Jesus. Not because Jesus provides us with the best system, but because Jesus is simply the Way, the Truth, and the Life.

CPSIA information can be obtained
at www.ICGtesting.com
Printed in the USA
JSHW040903040522
25545JS00002B/10